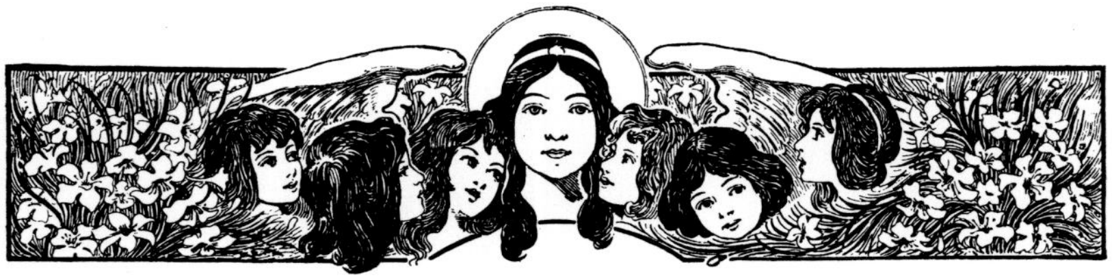

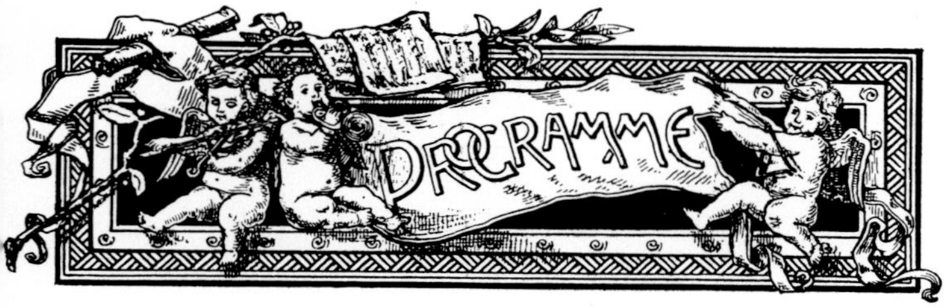
PROGRAMME

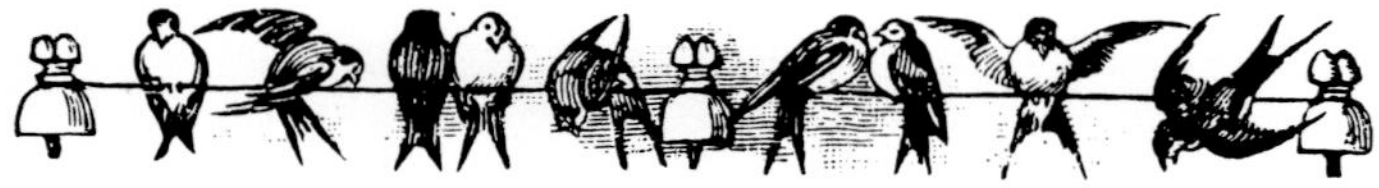

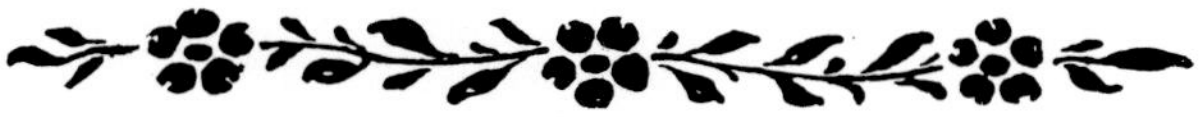

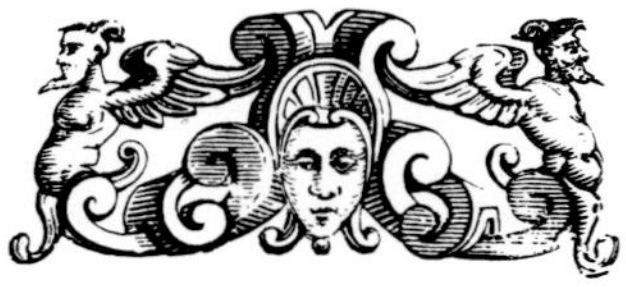

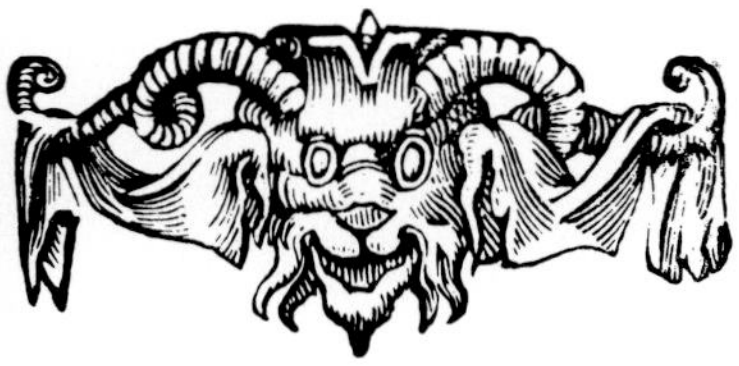

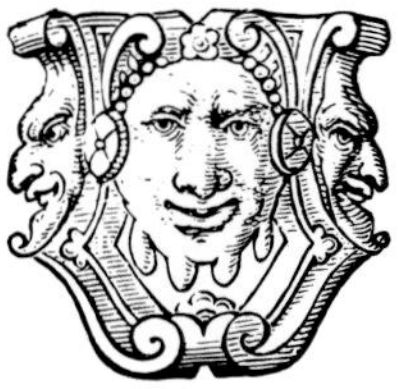

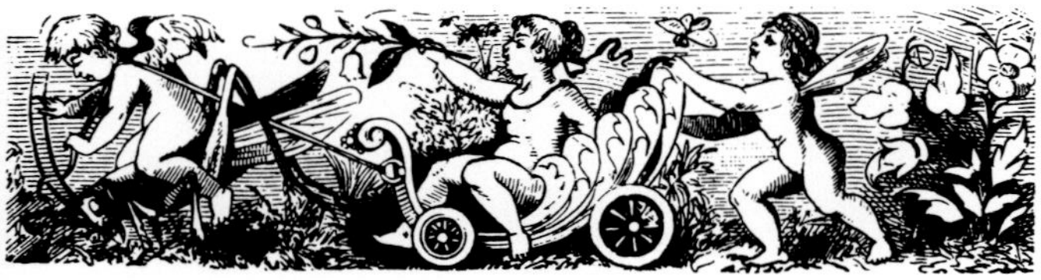

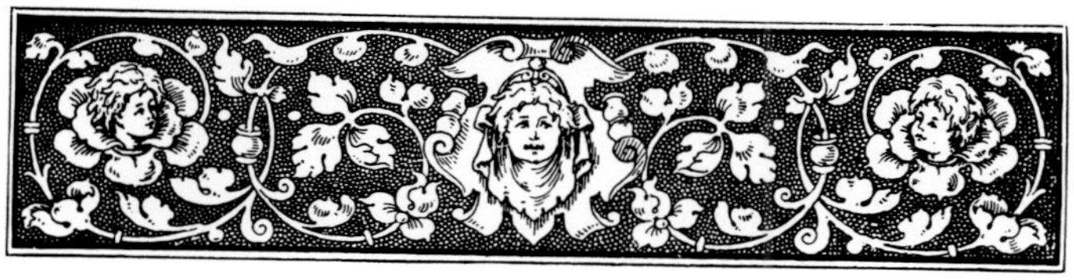

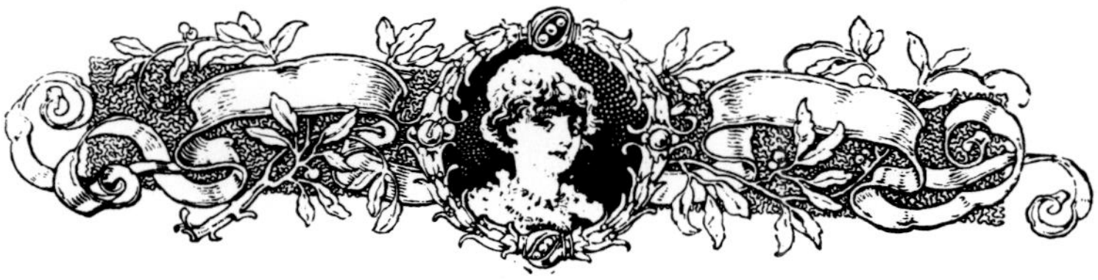

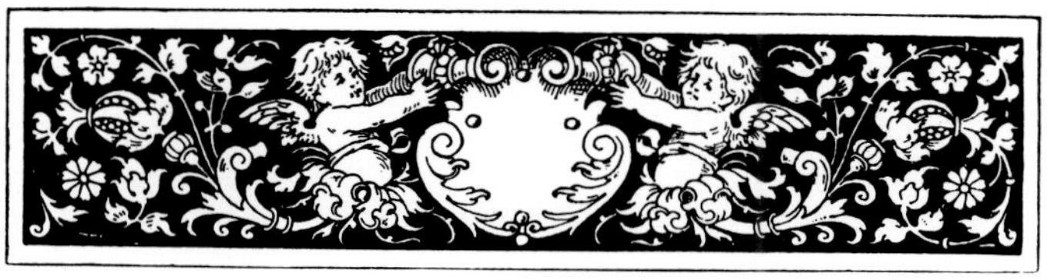

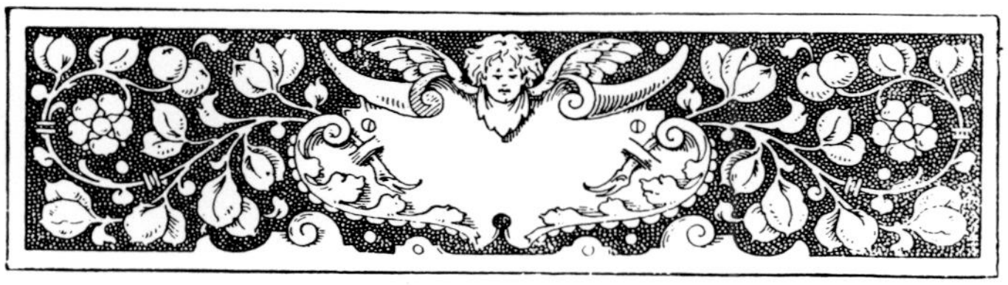

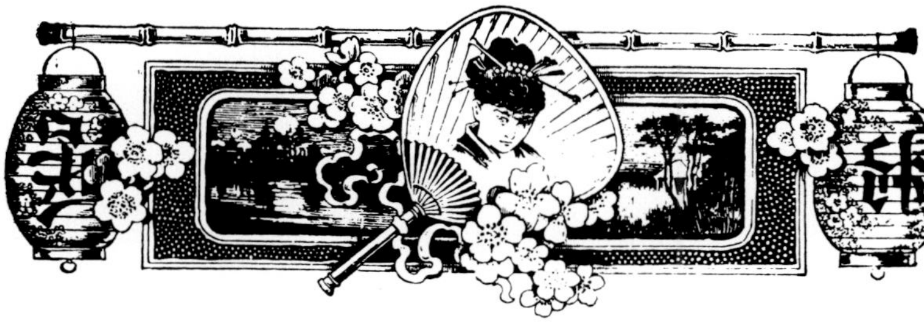

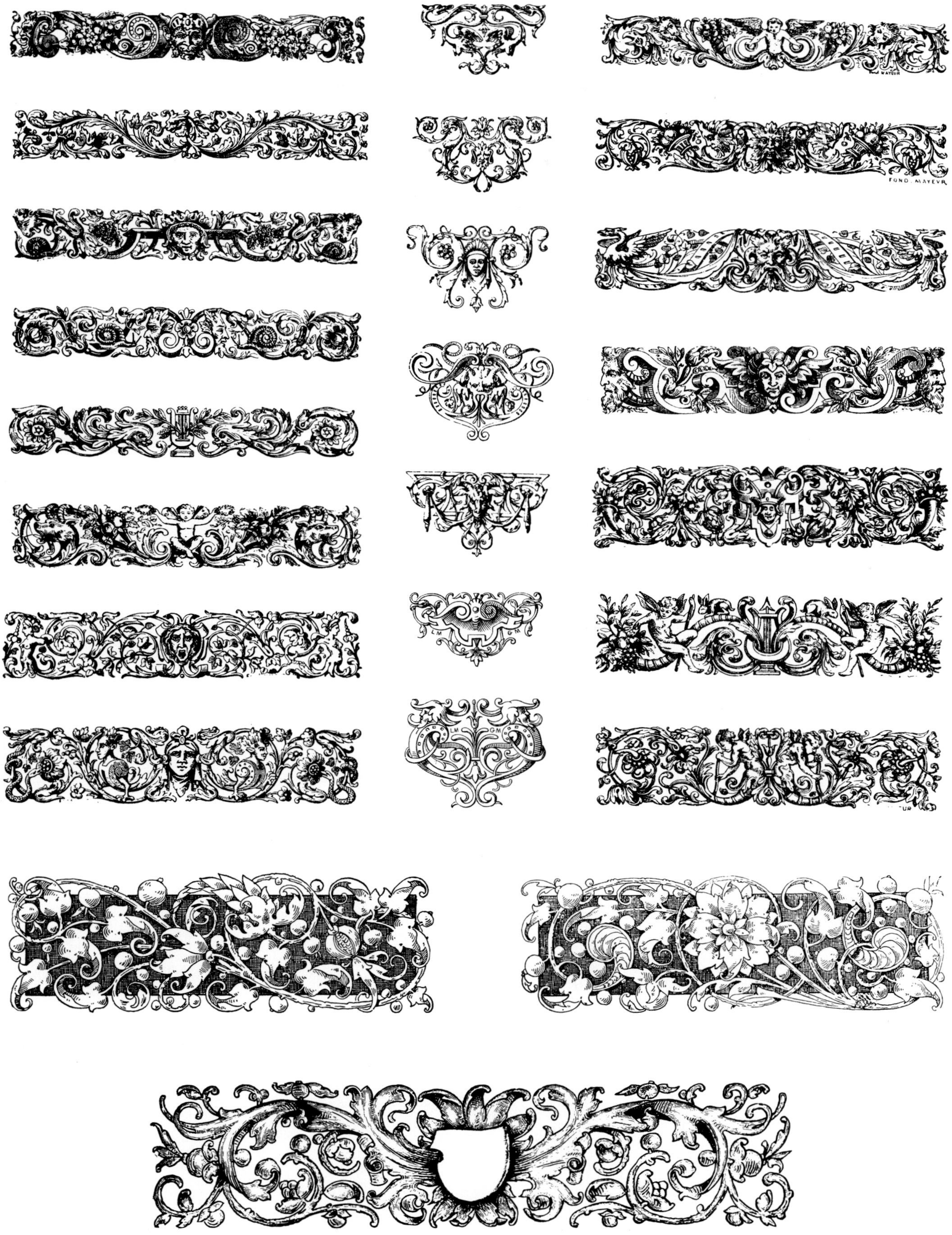
FOND. MAYEUR

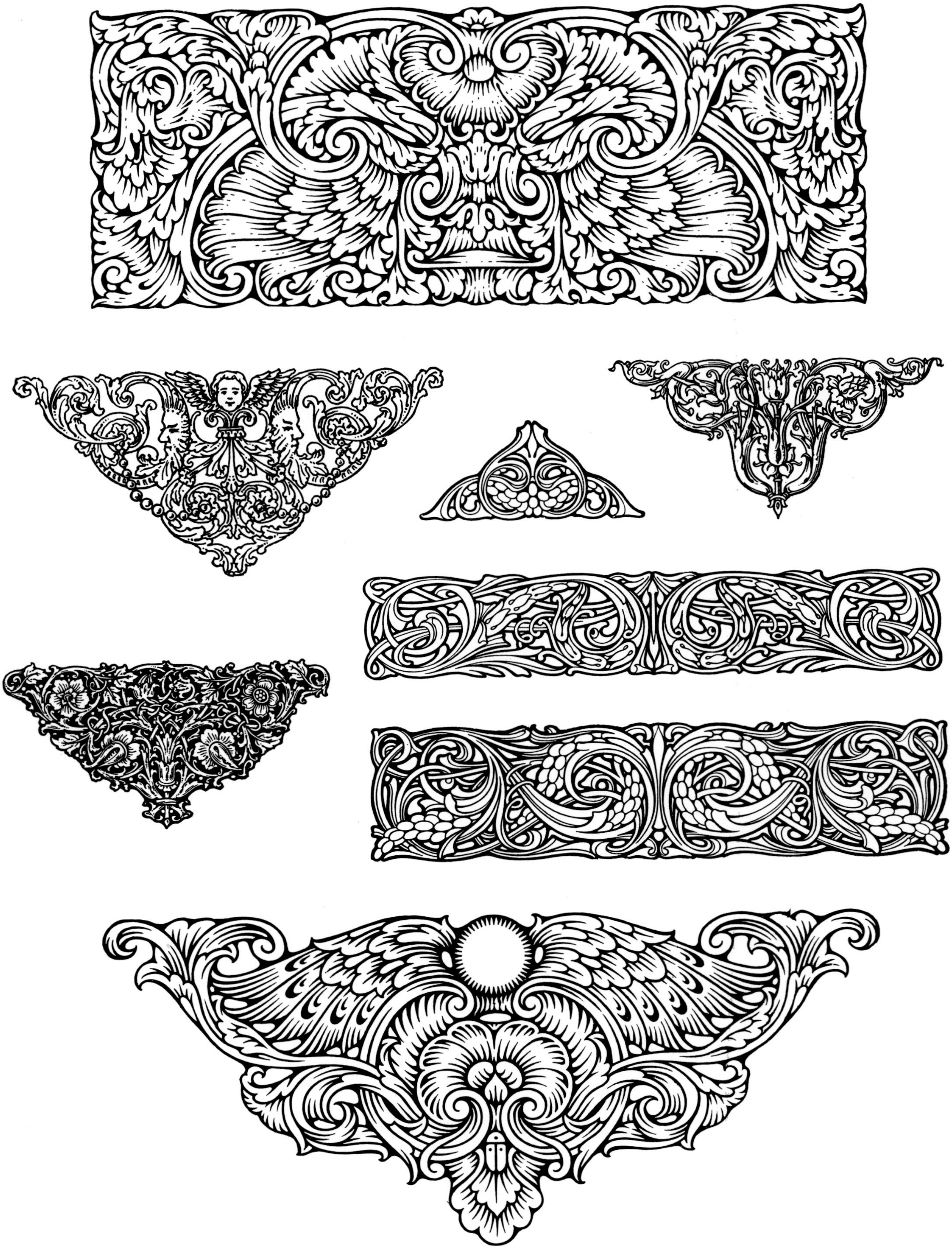

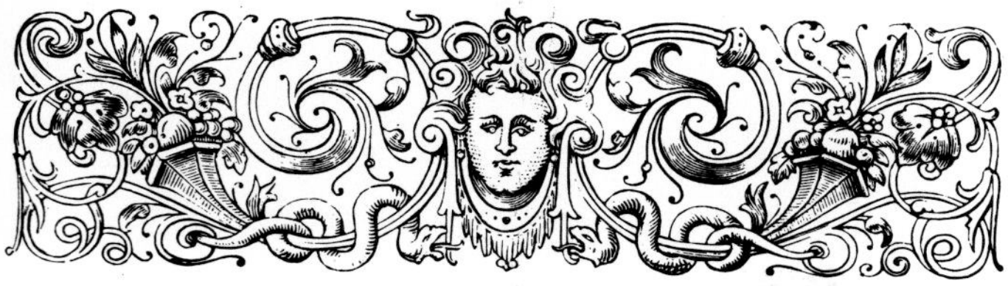
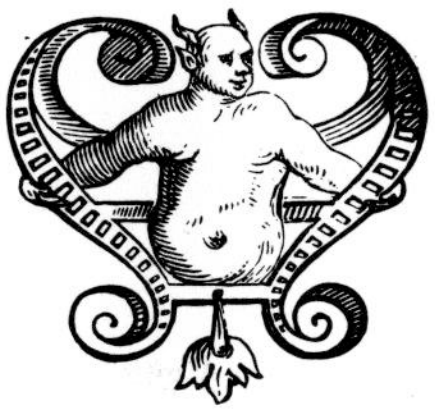
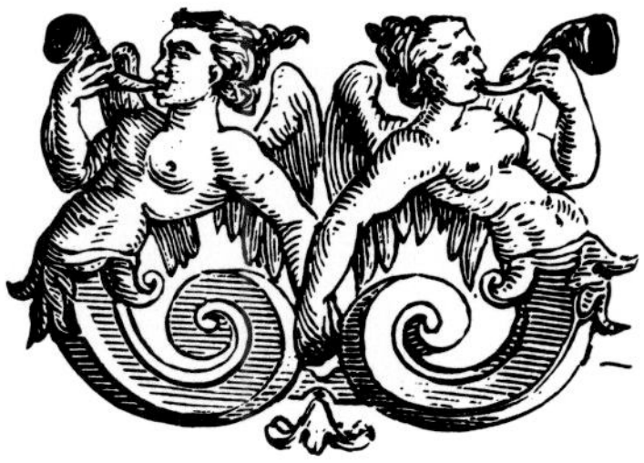
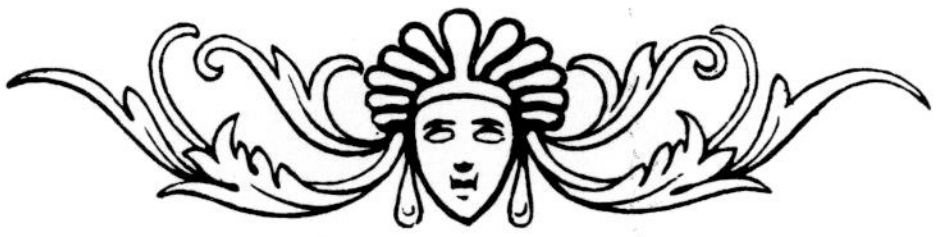

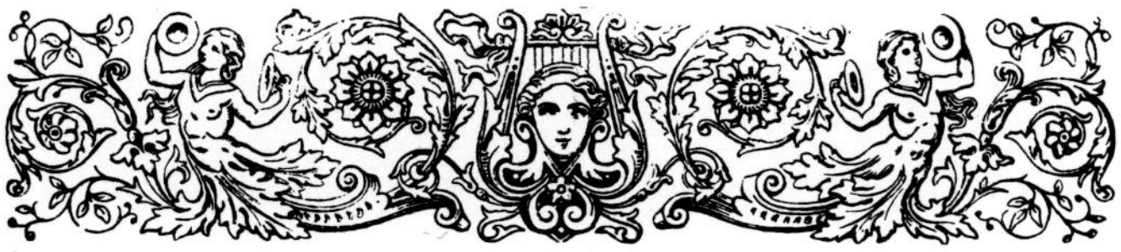

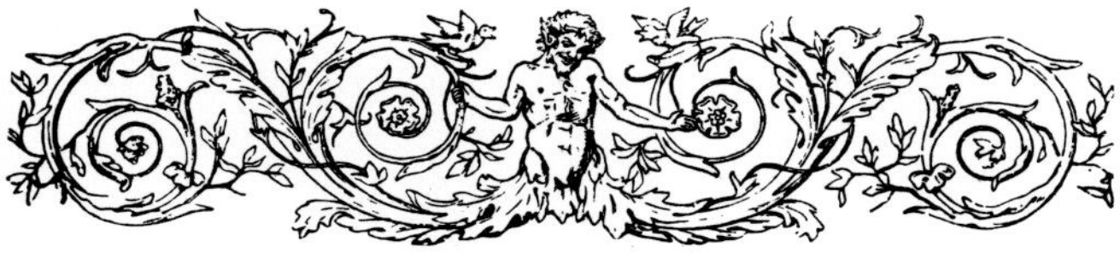
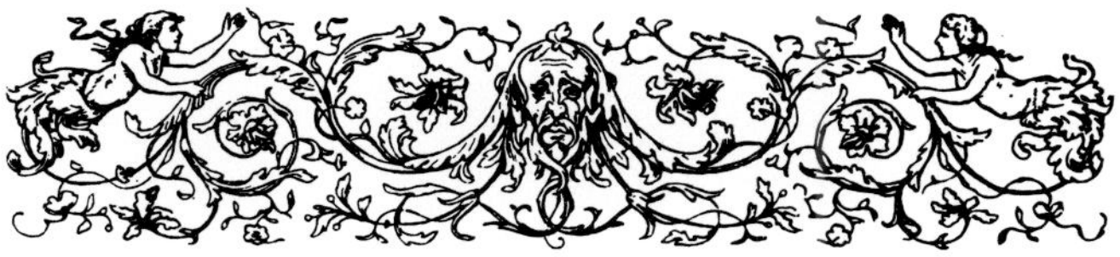
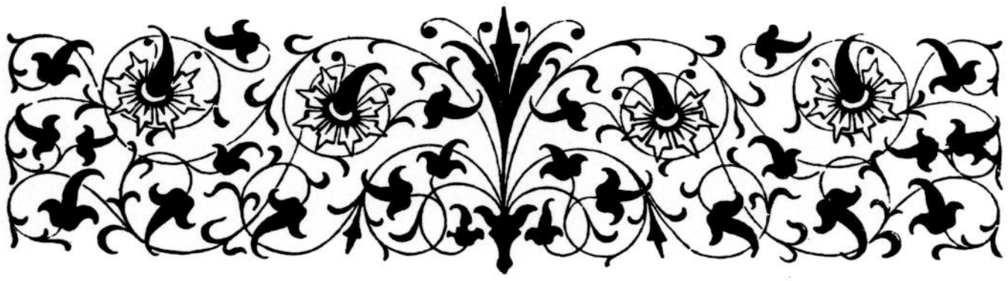
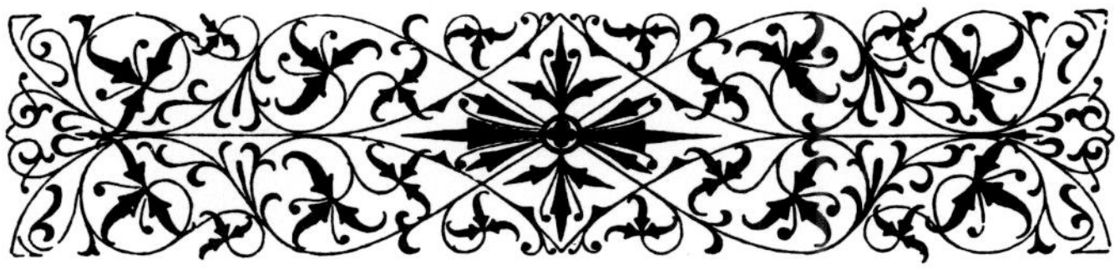
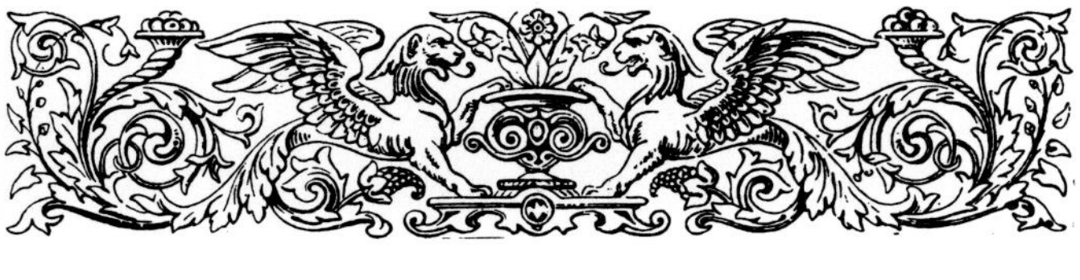
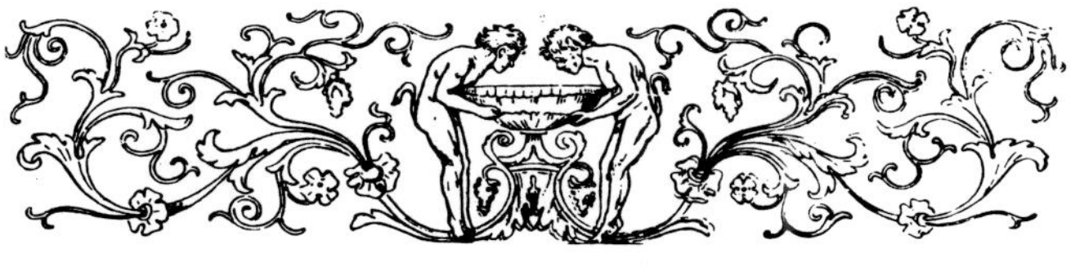
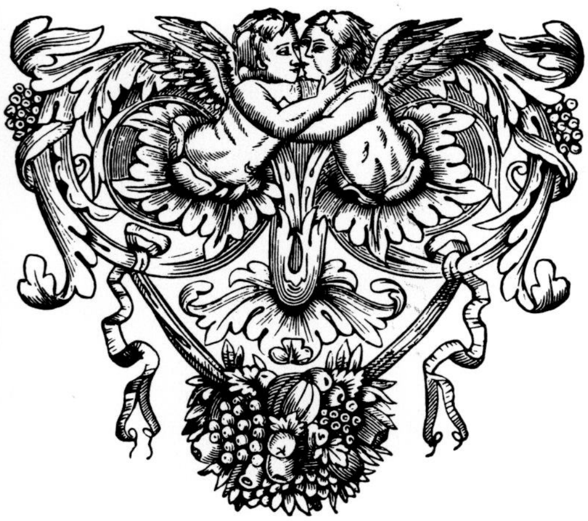
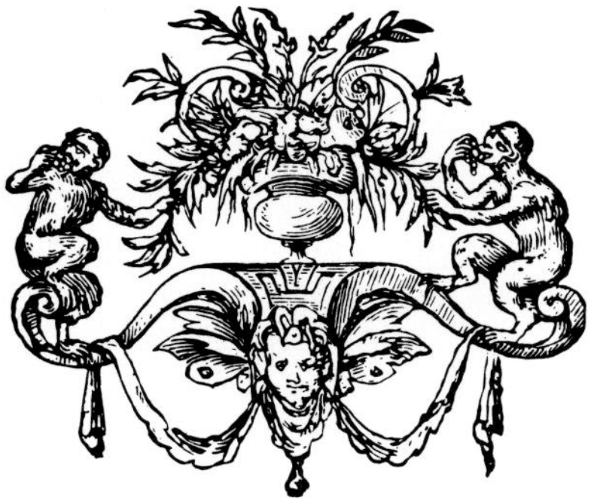
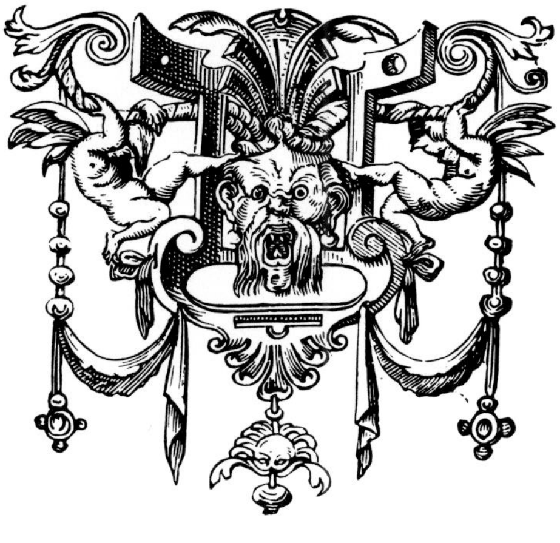

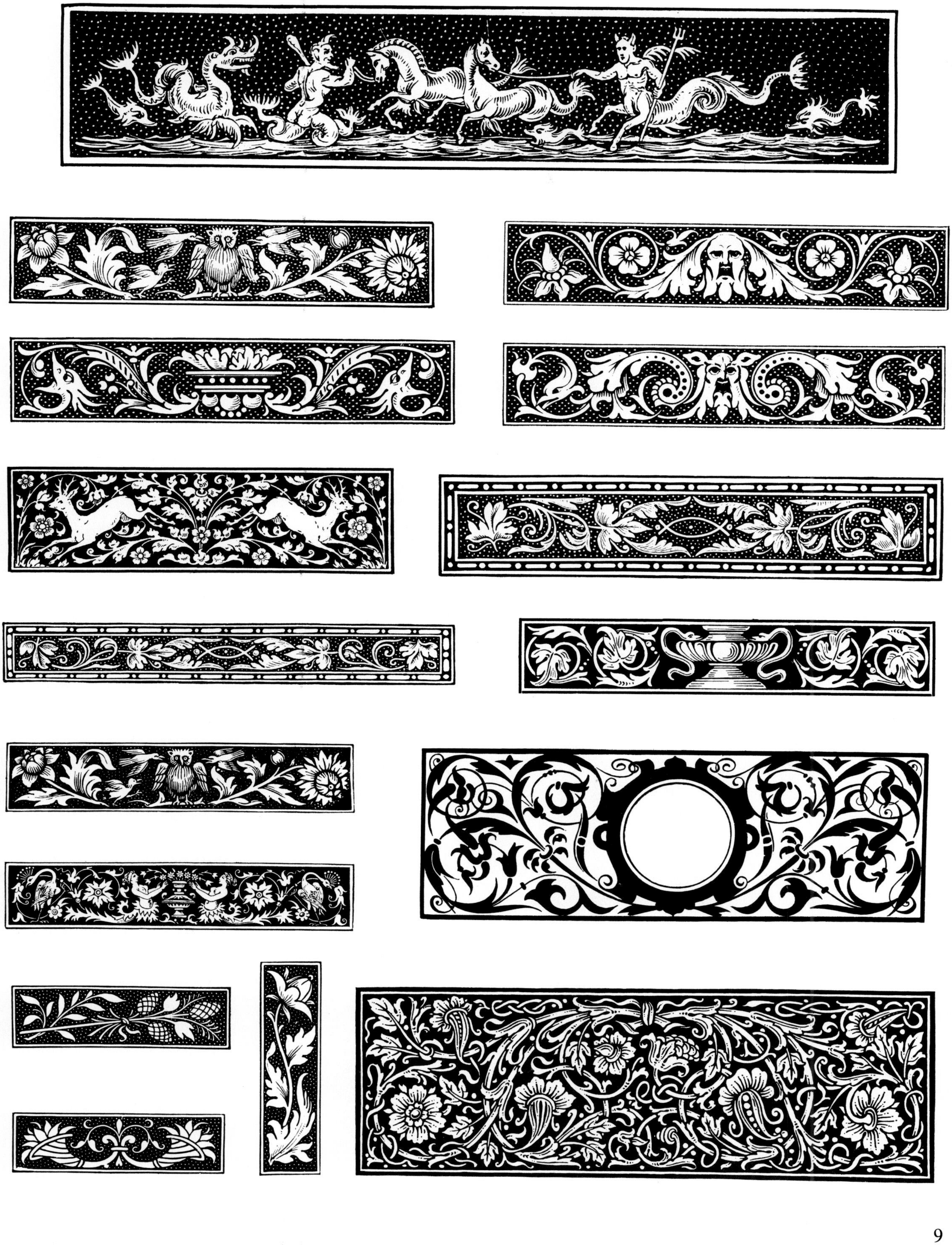

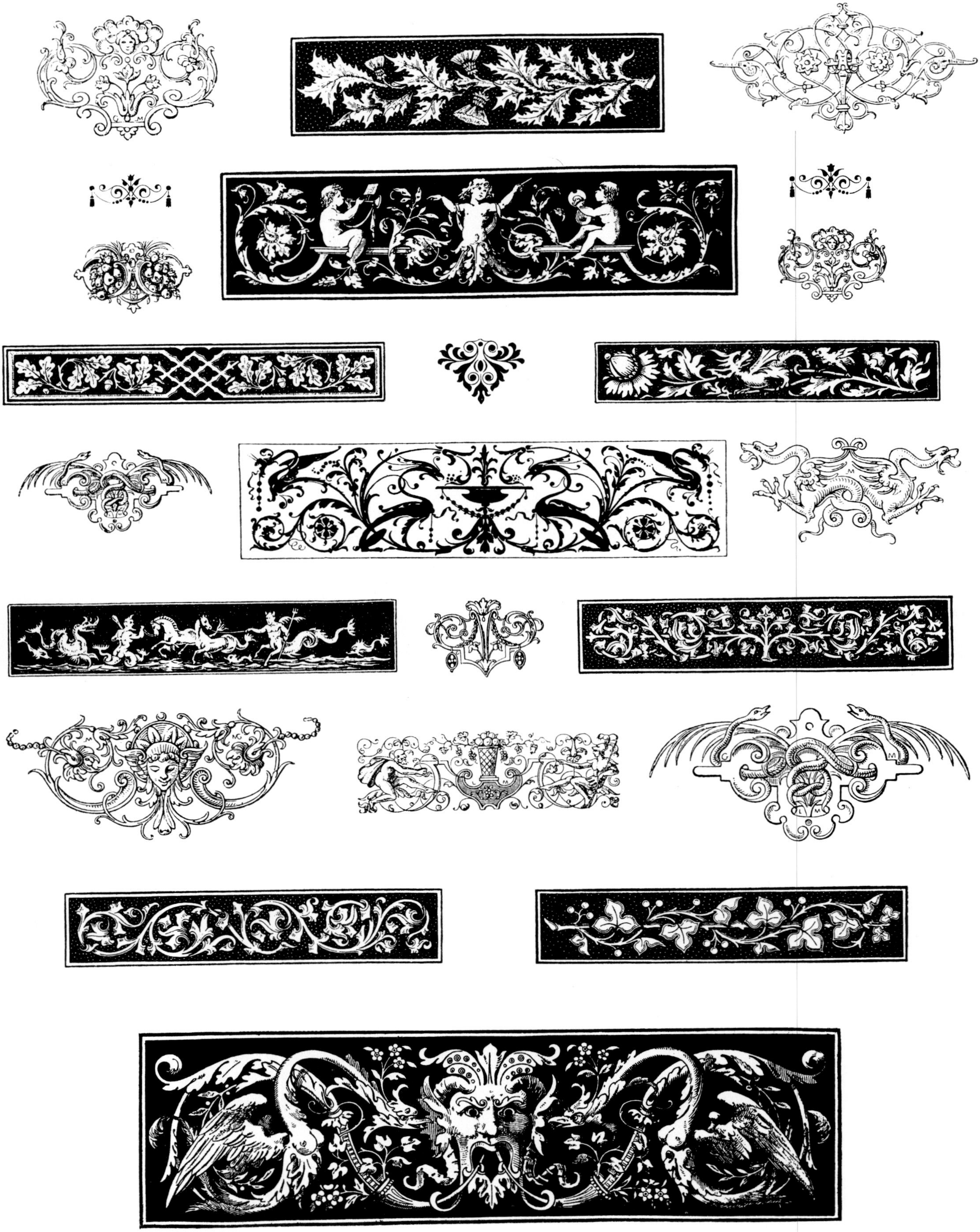

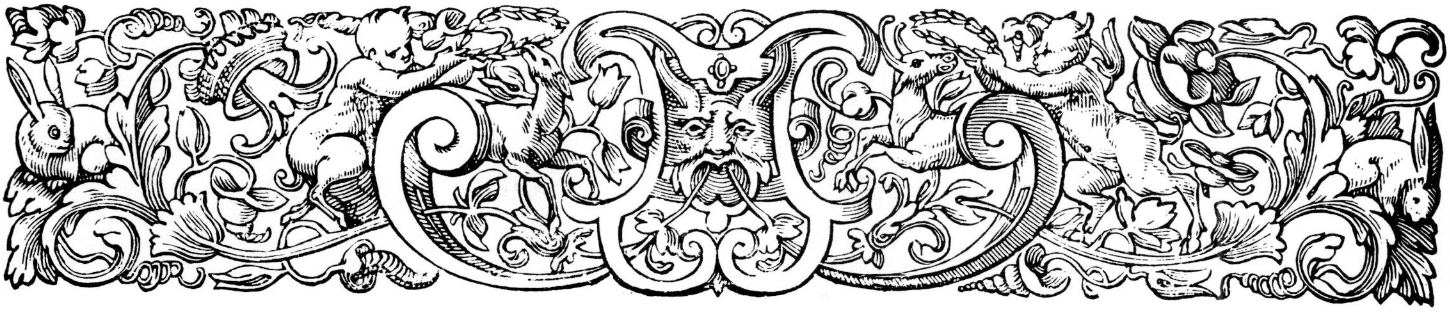

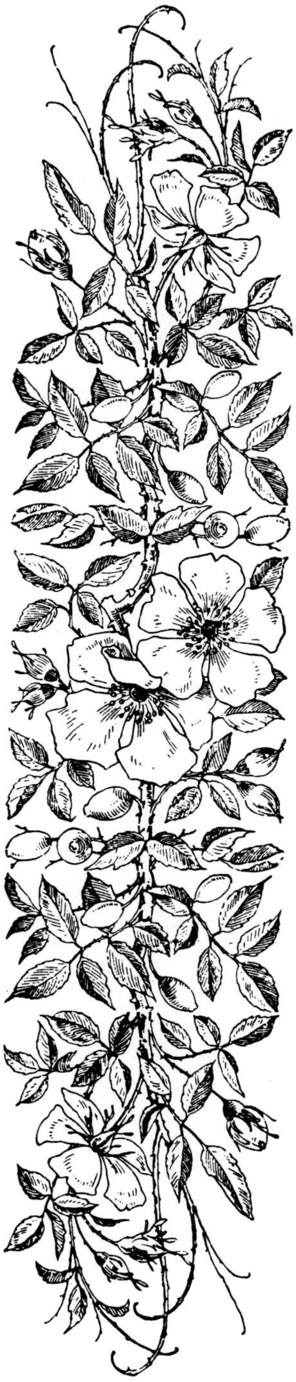

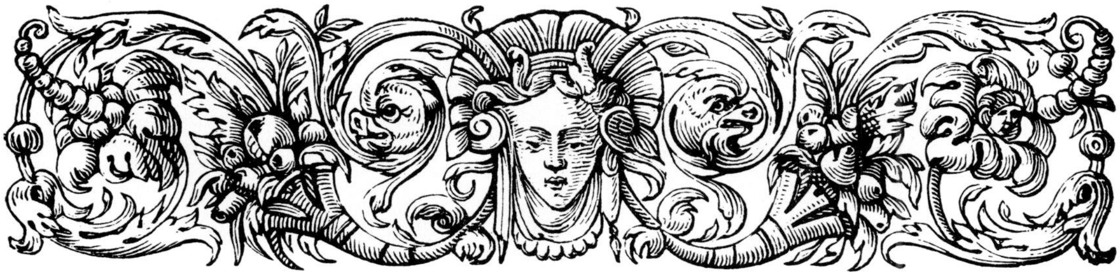

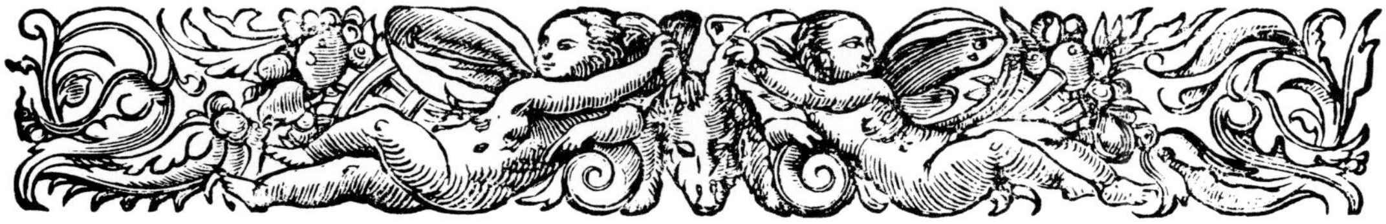

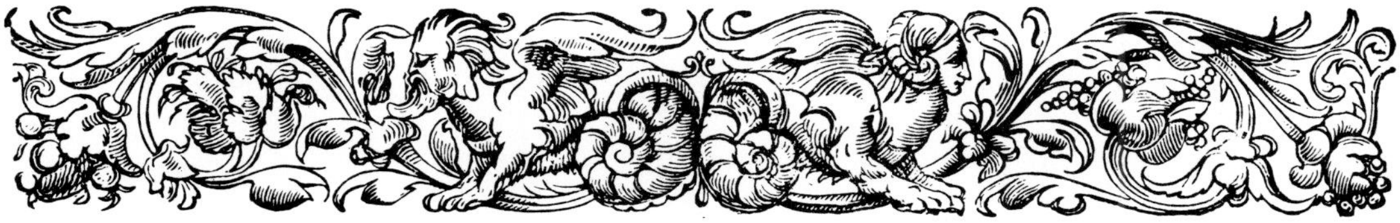

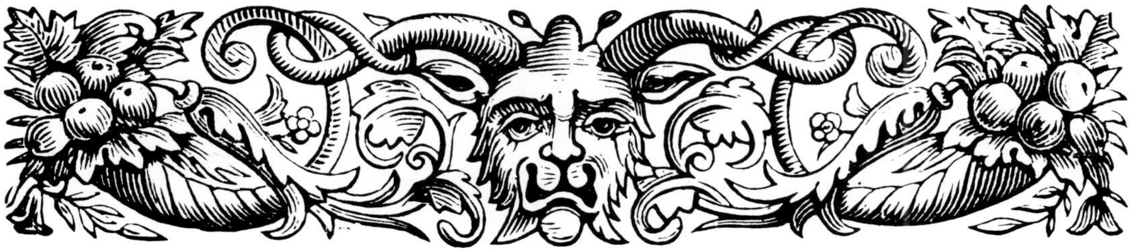

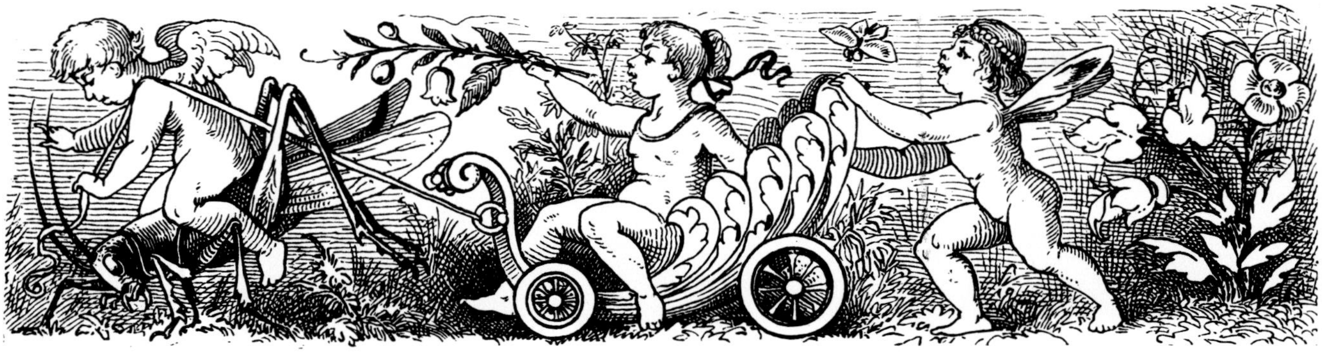

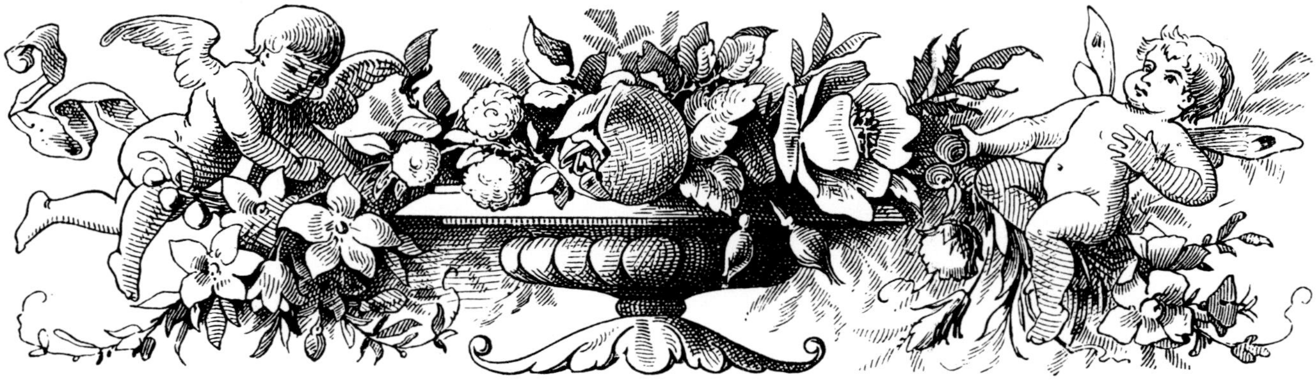

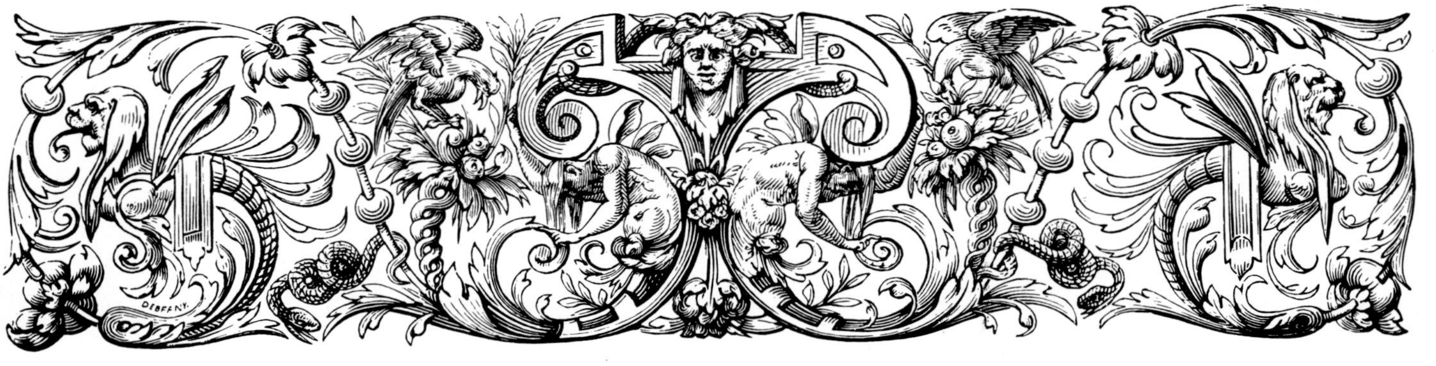

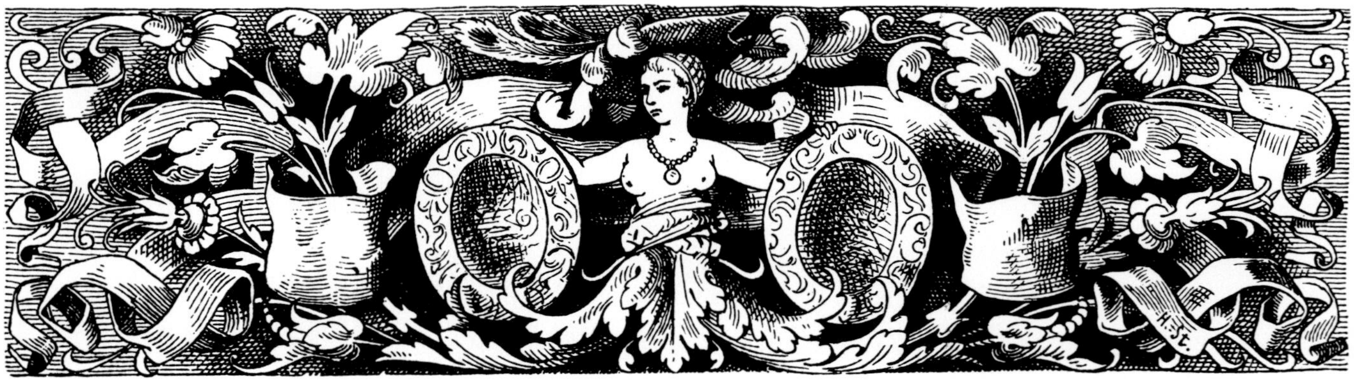

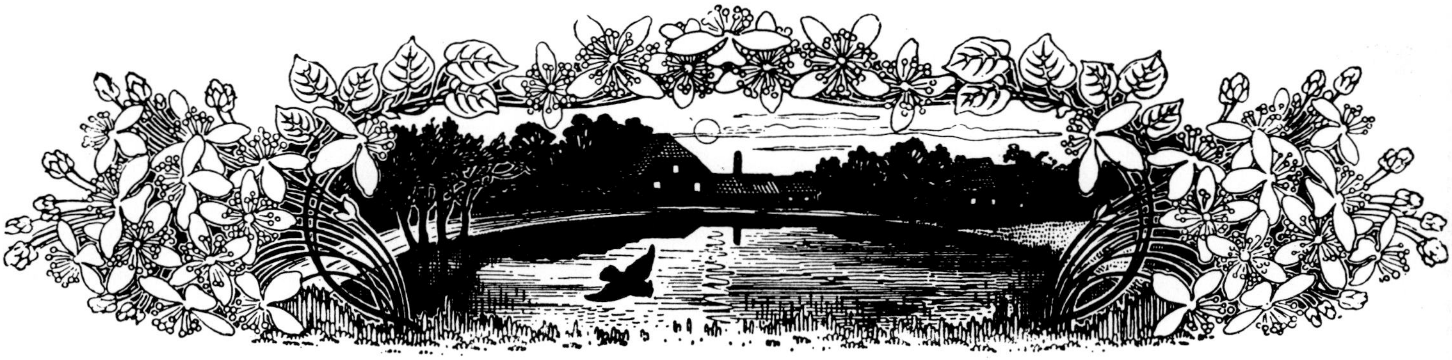

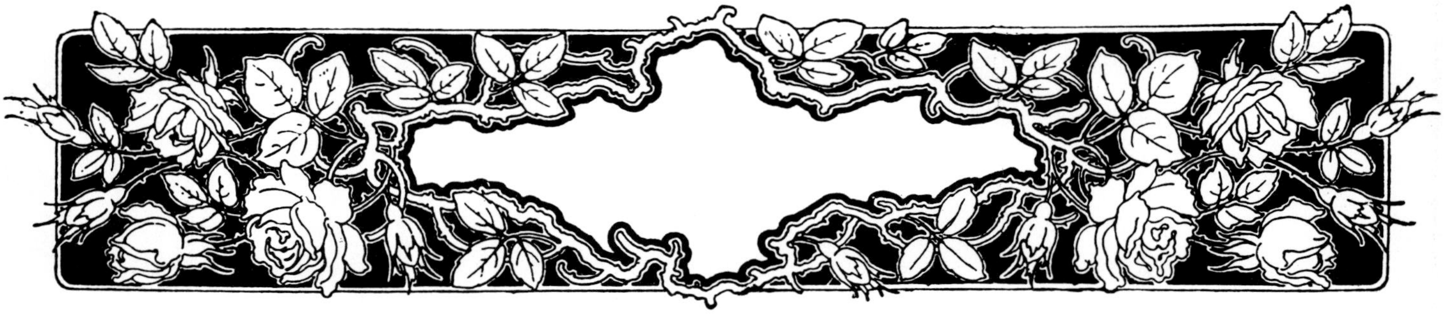

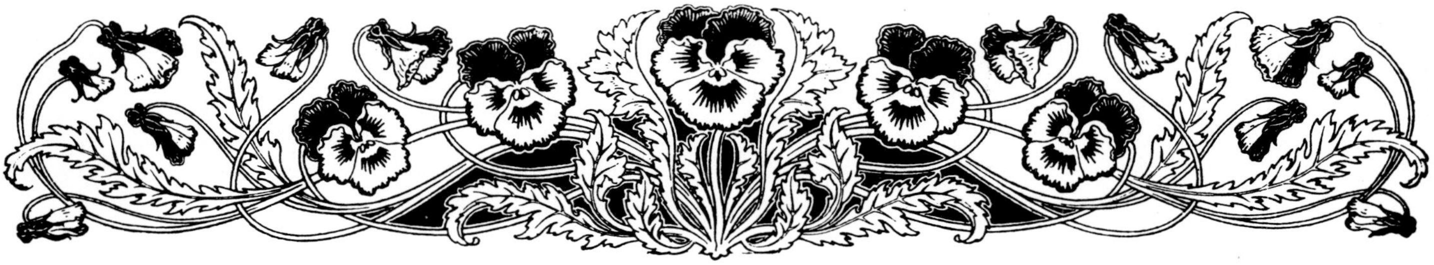

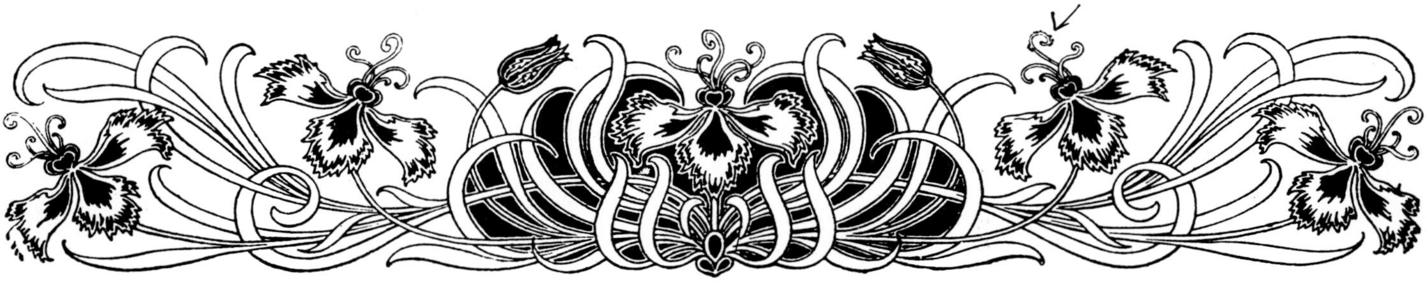

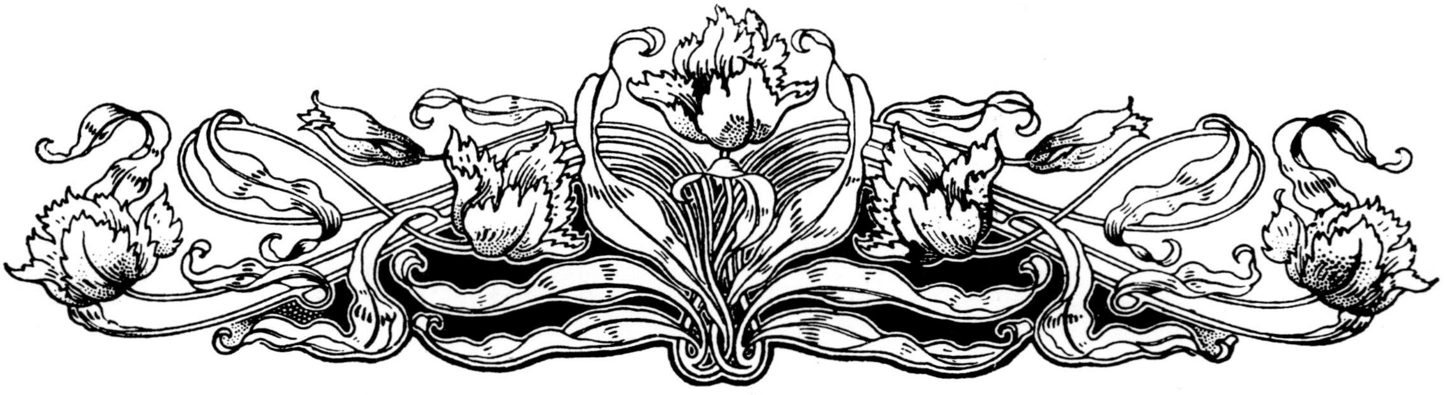

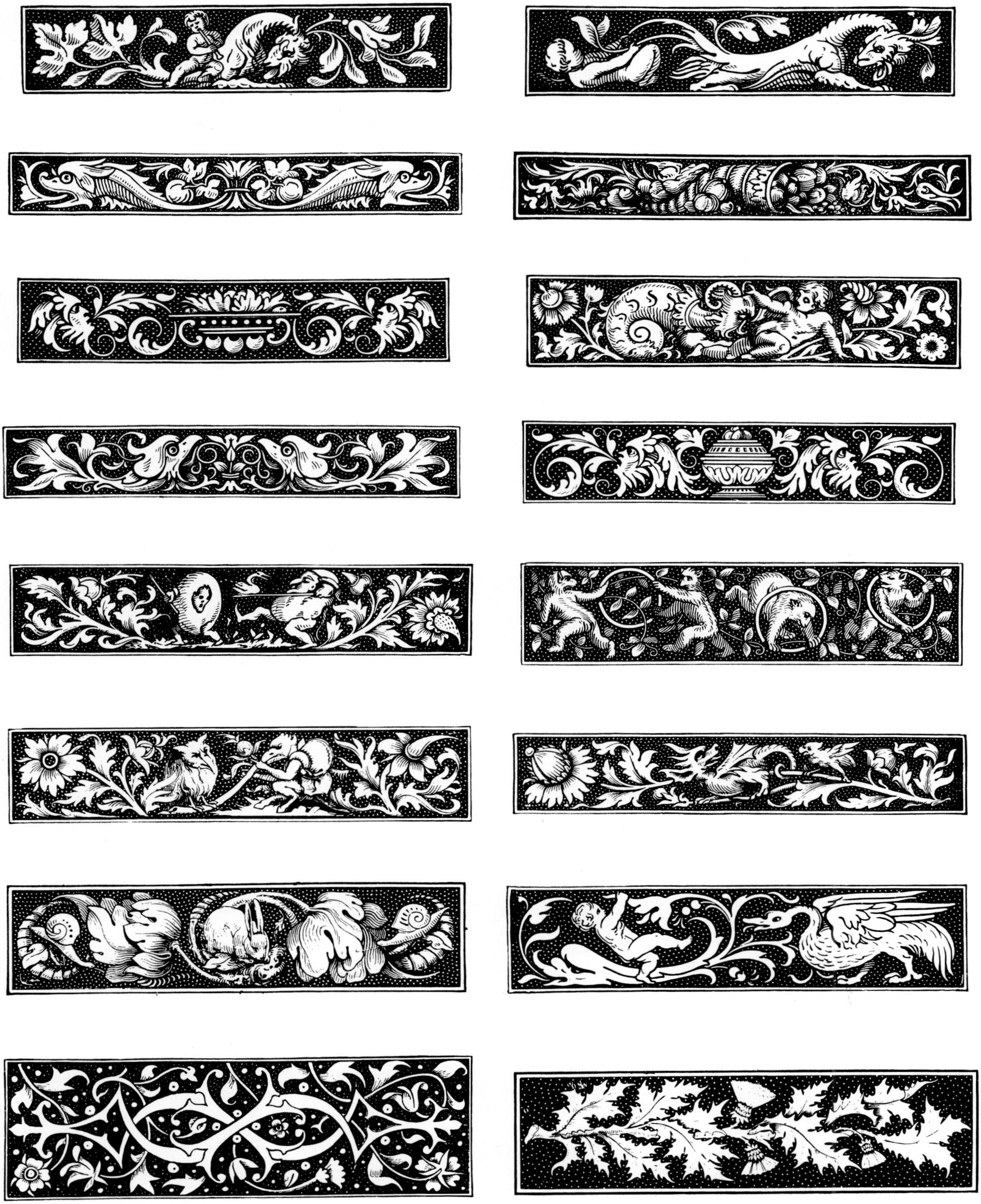

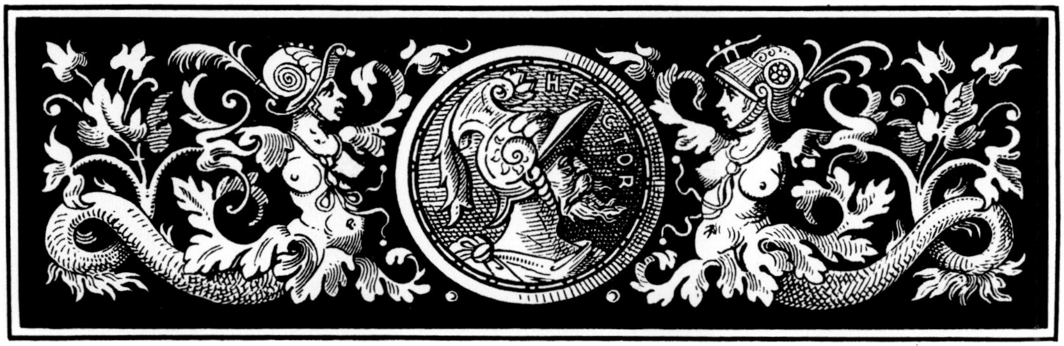
HECTOR

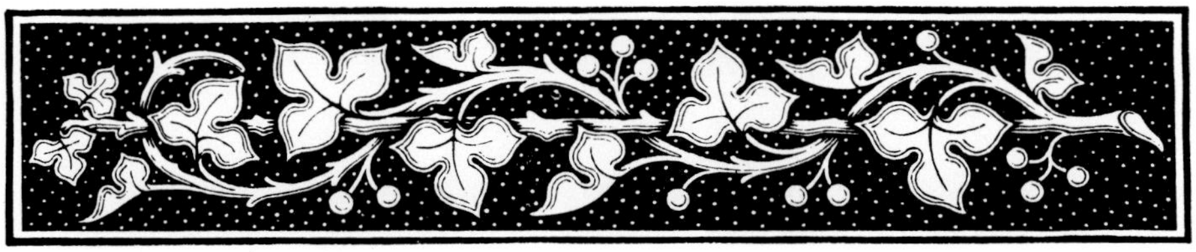

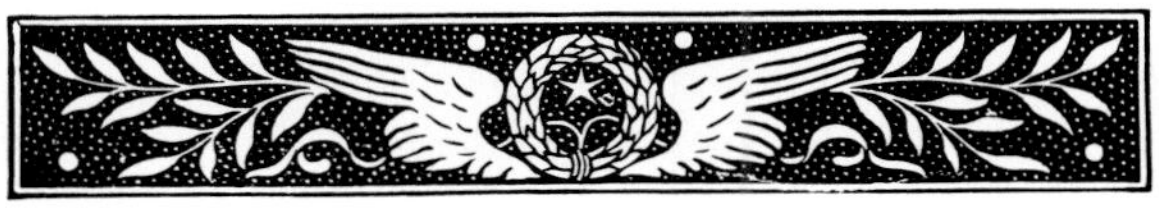

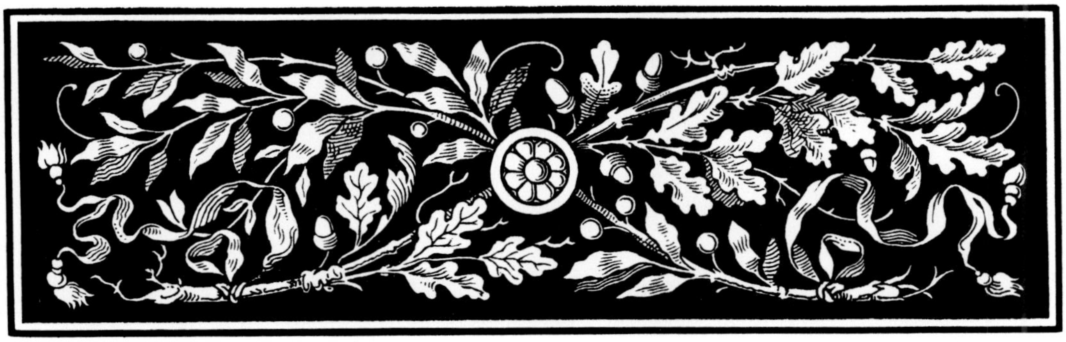

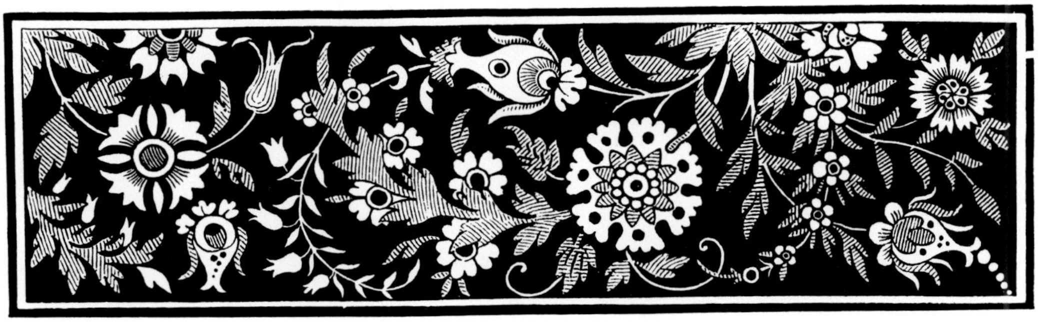

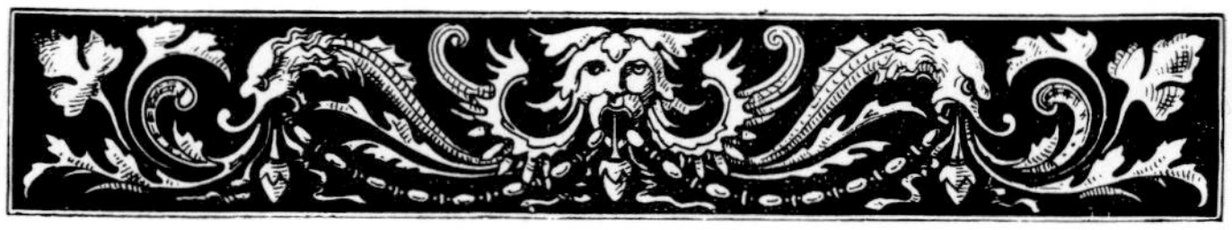
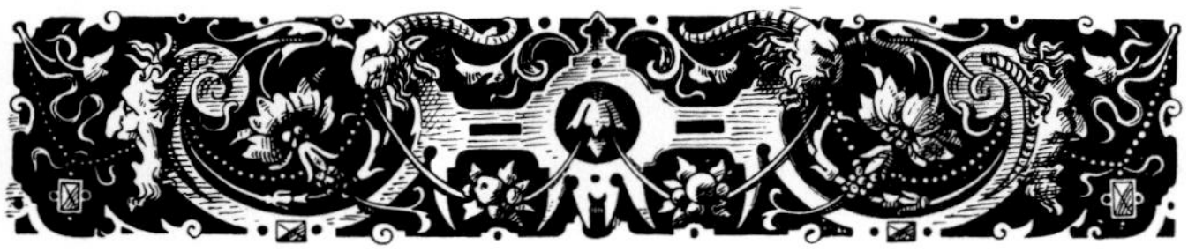

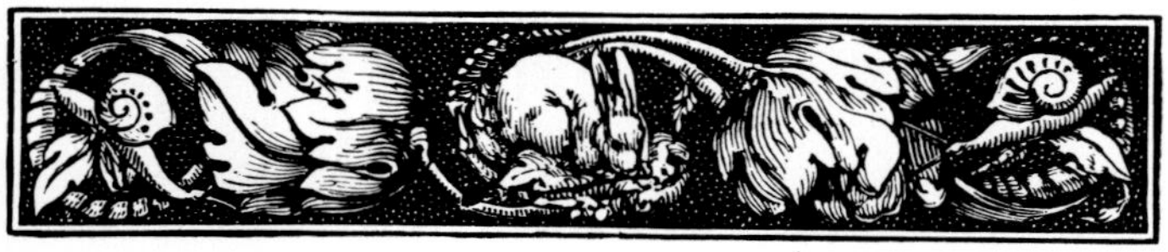
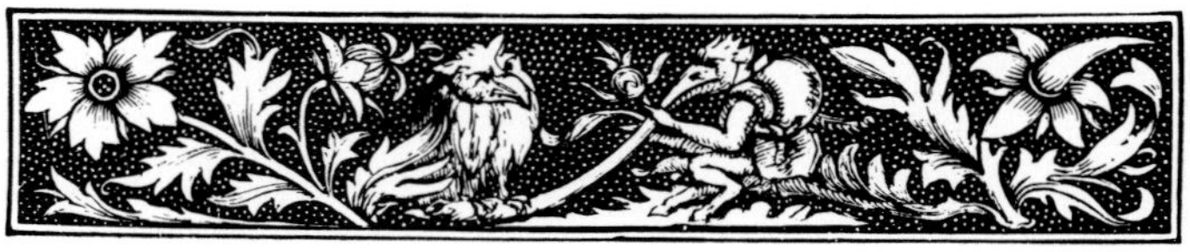
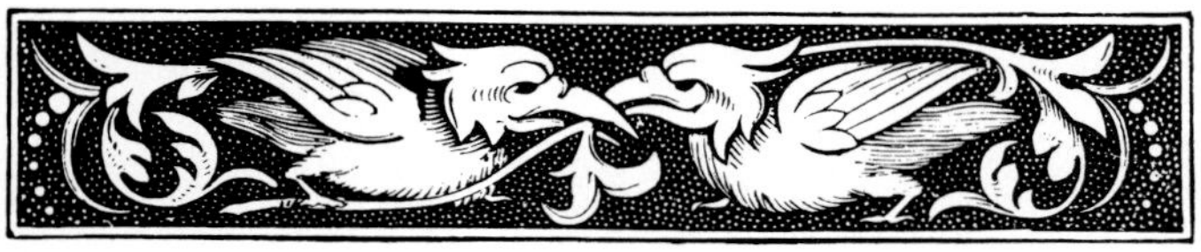
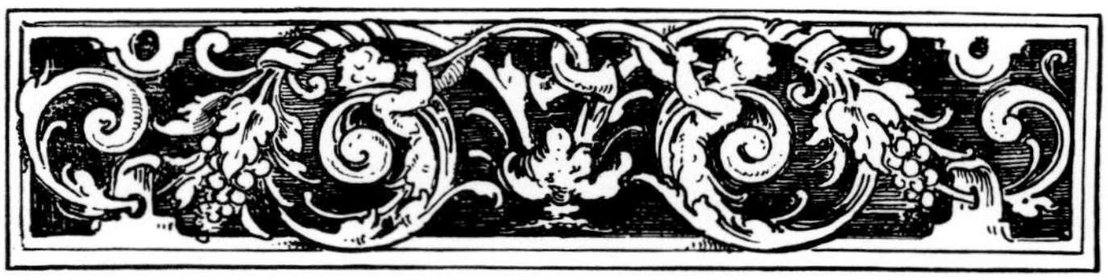
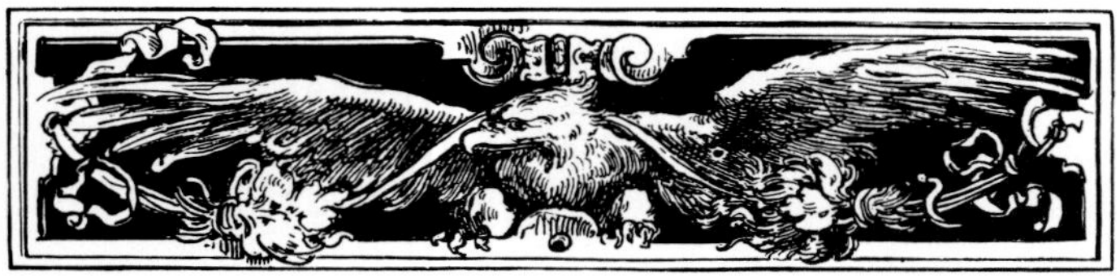
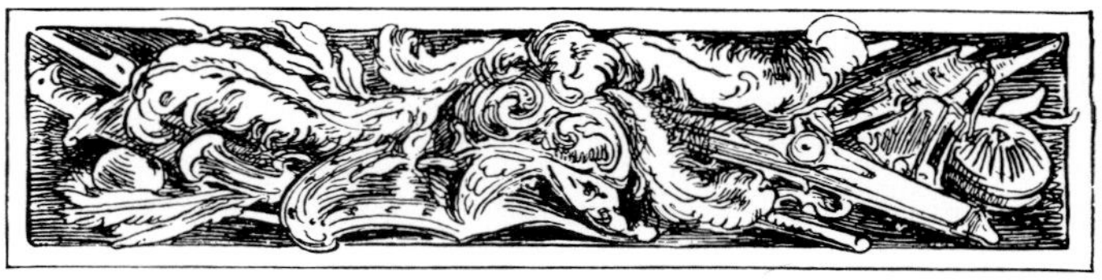
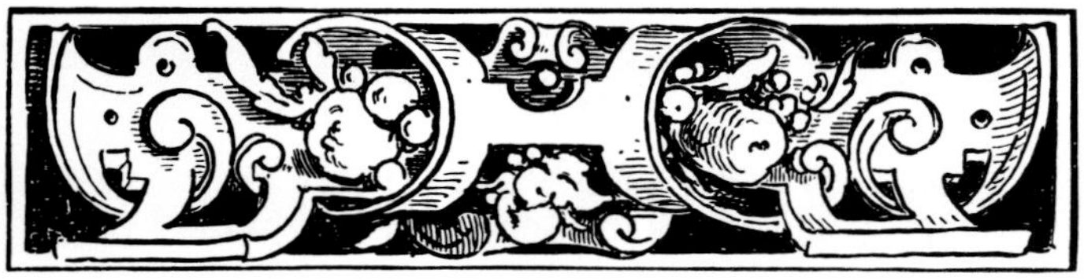
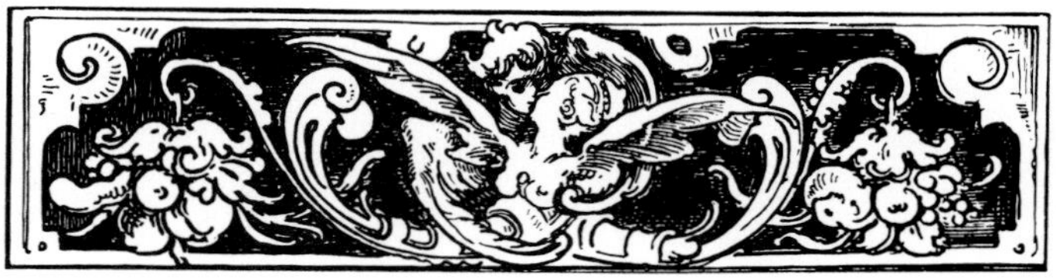
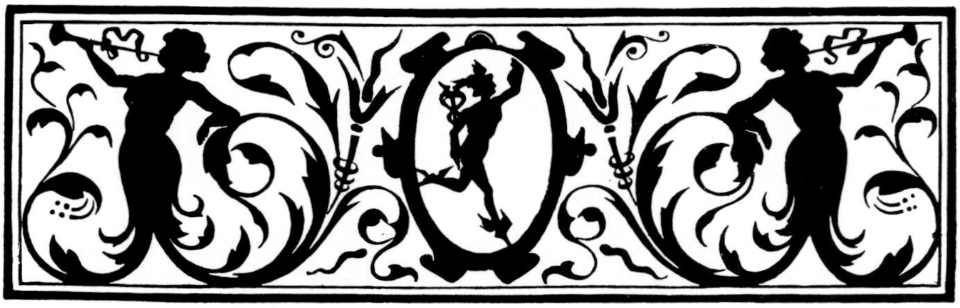

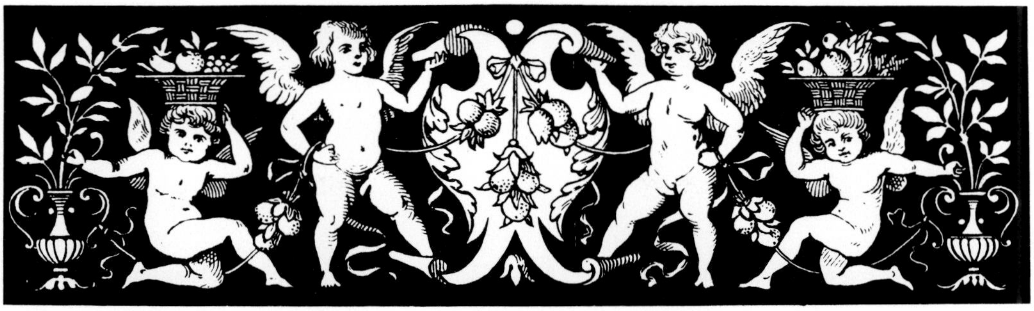

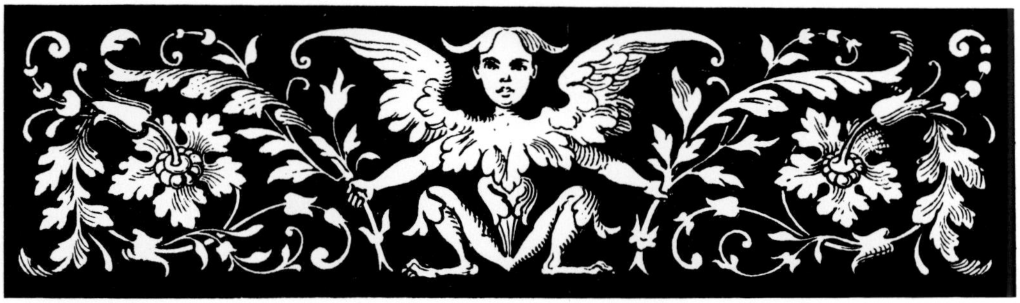

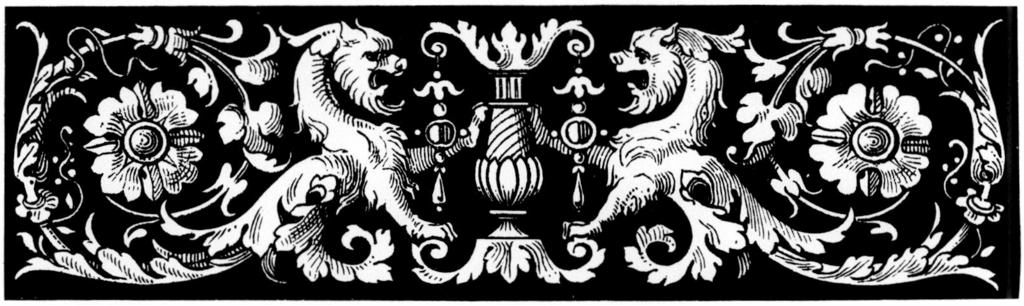

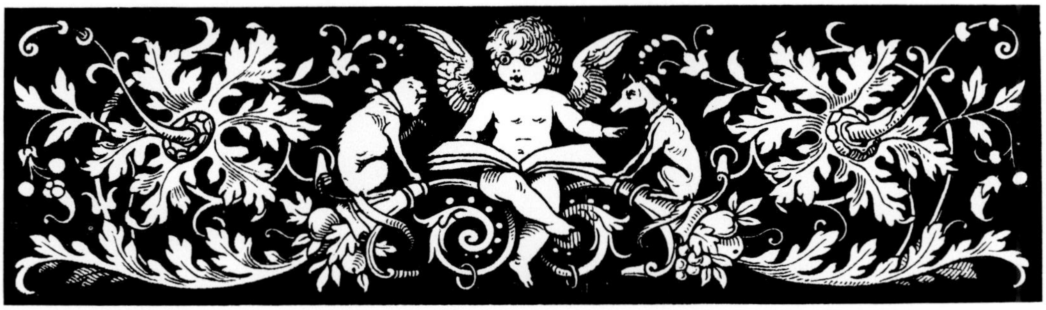

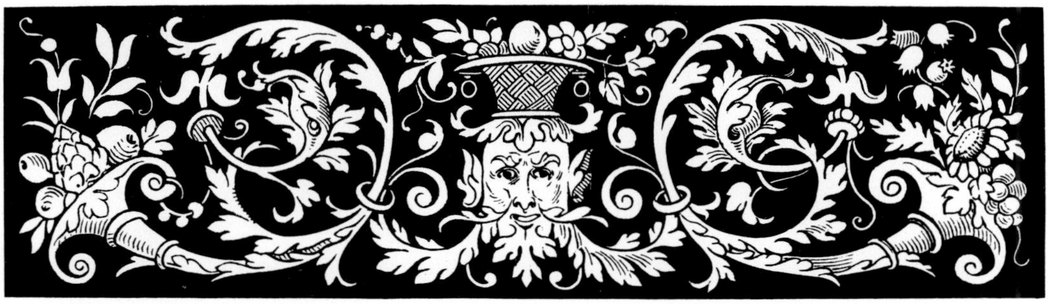

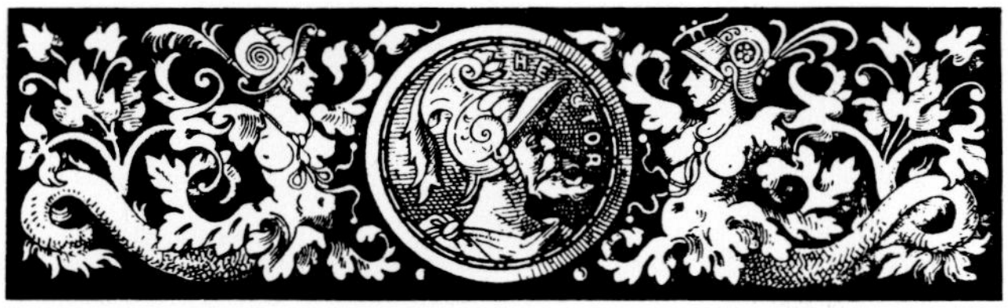
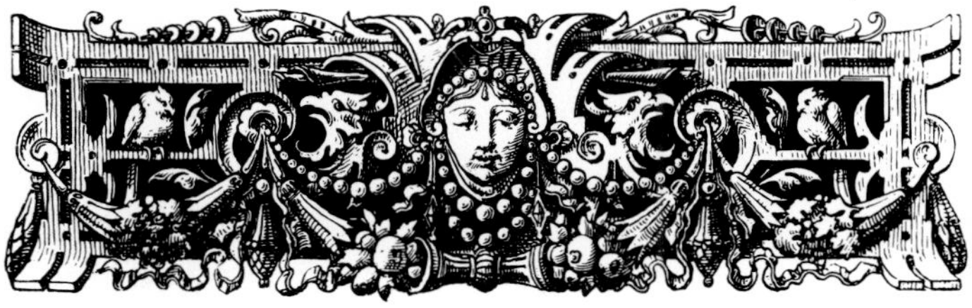

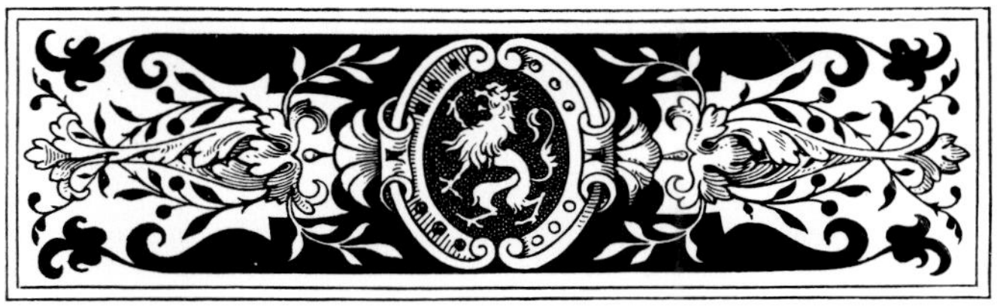
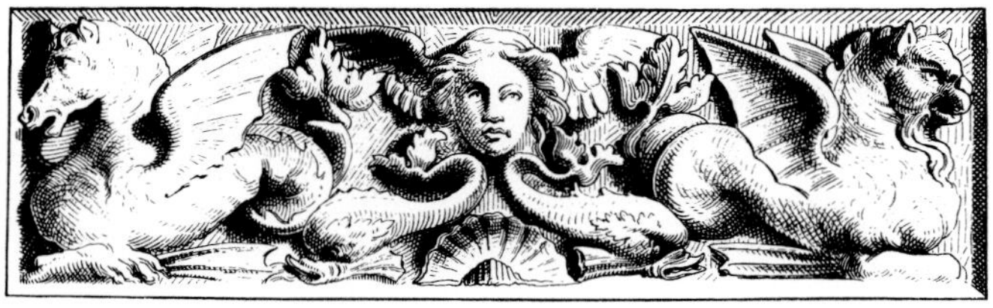
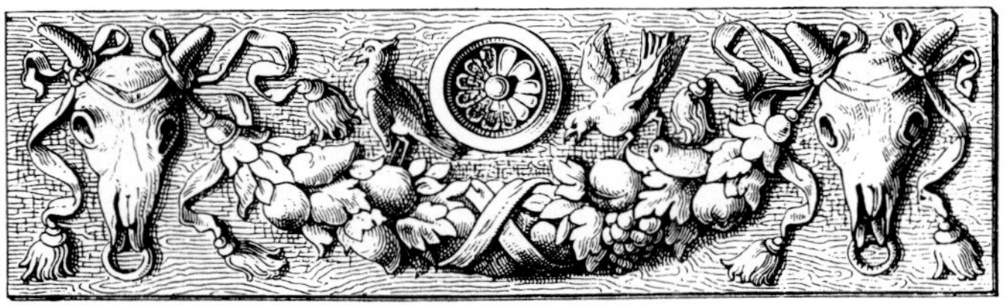
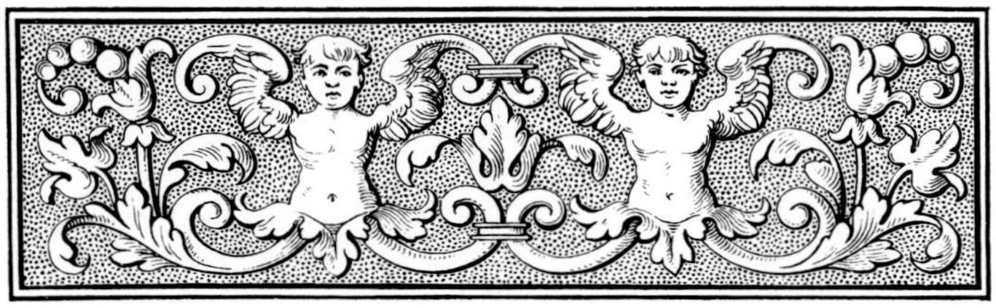
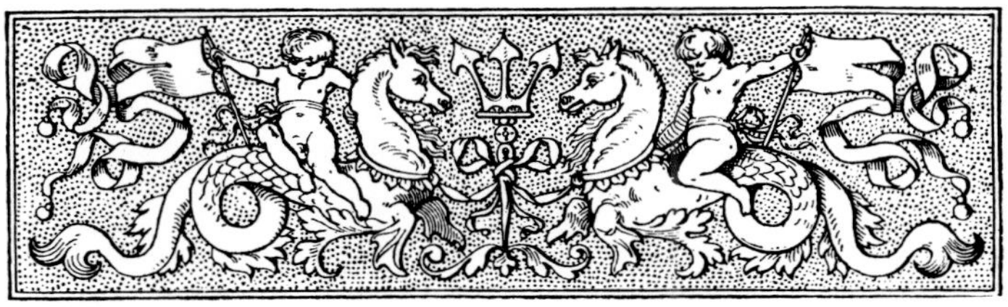
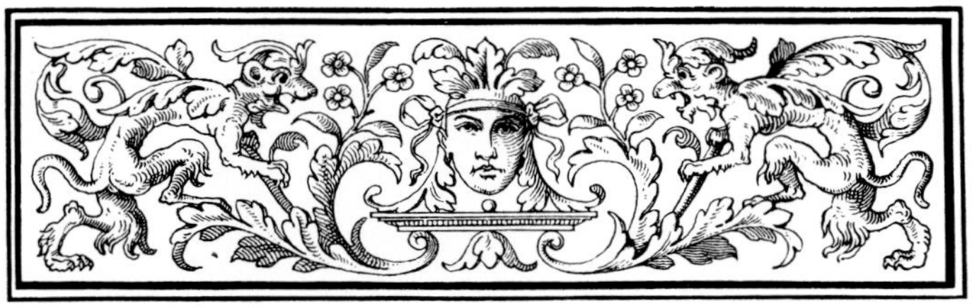

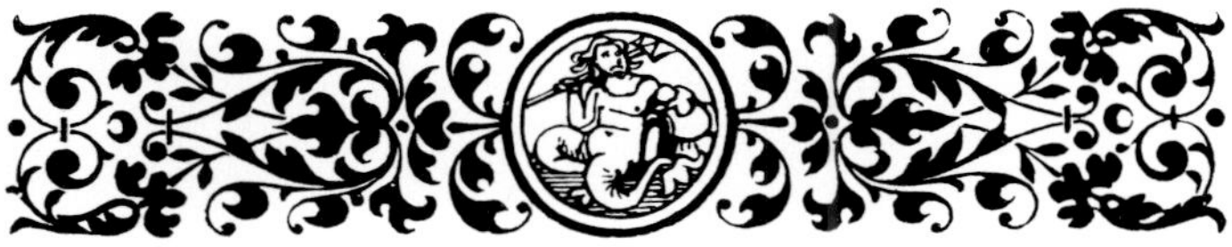

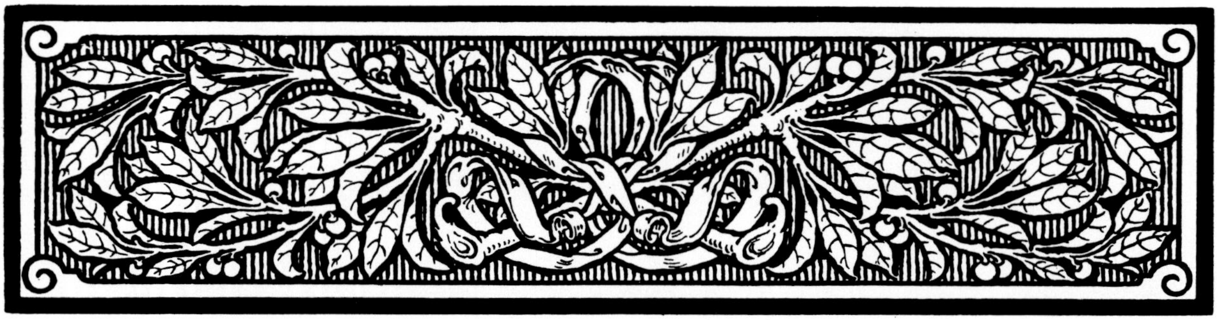

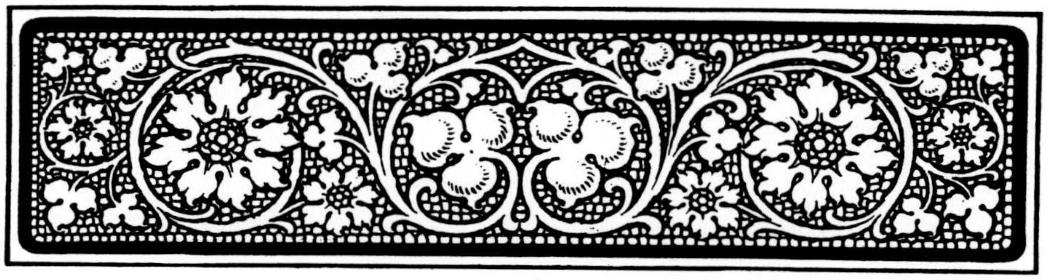

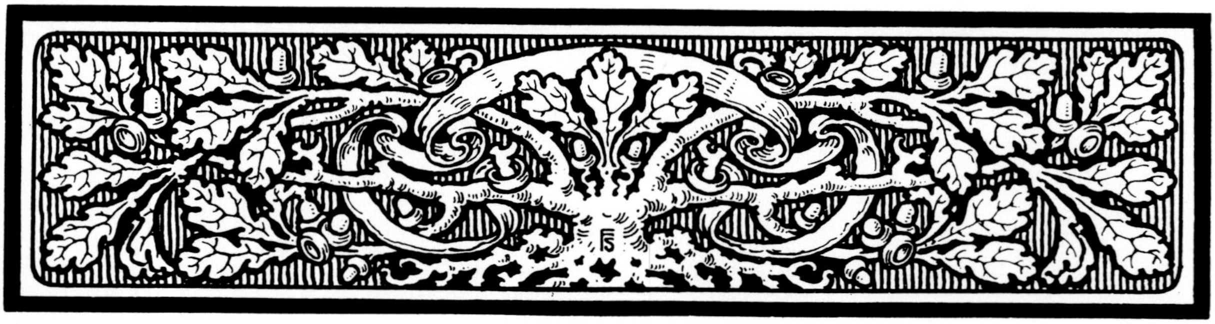

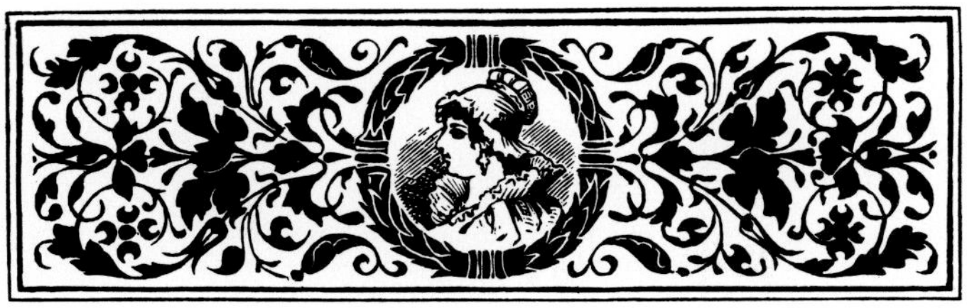

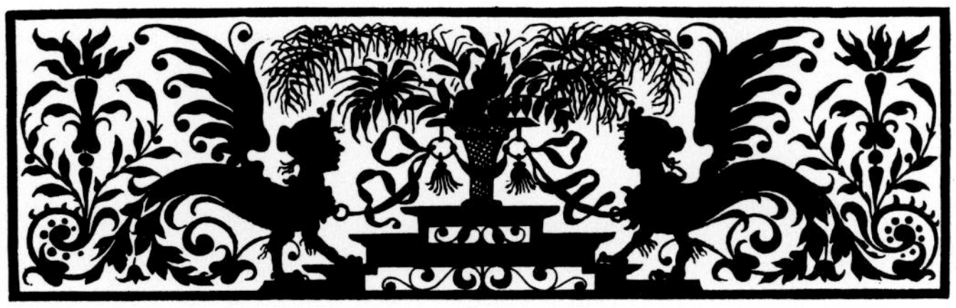

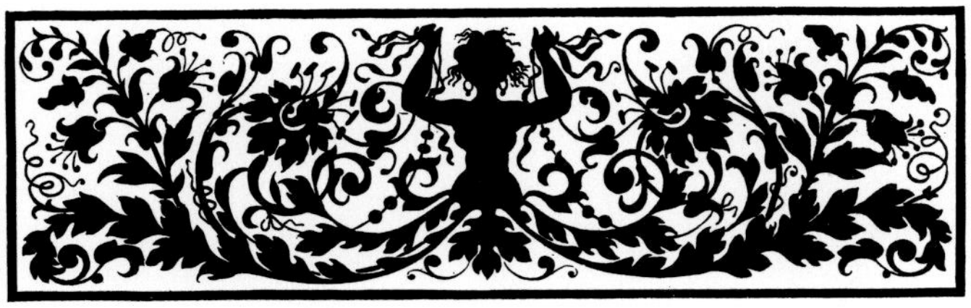

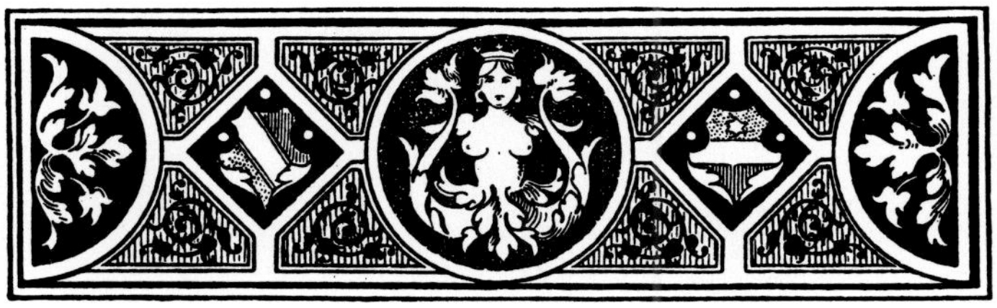

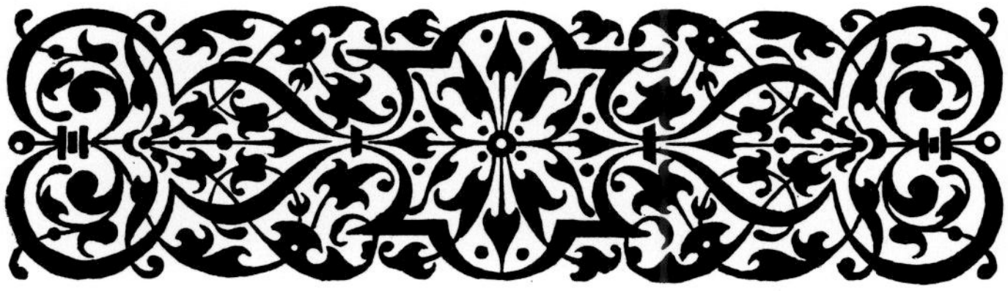

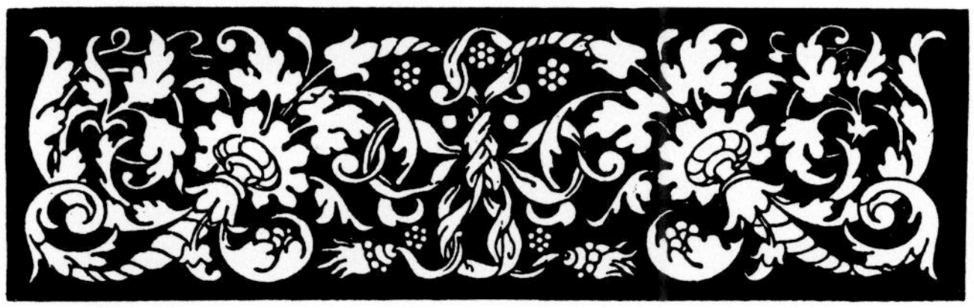

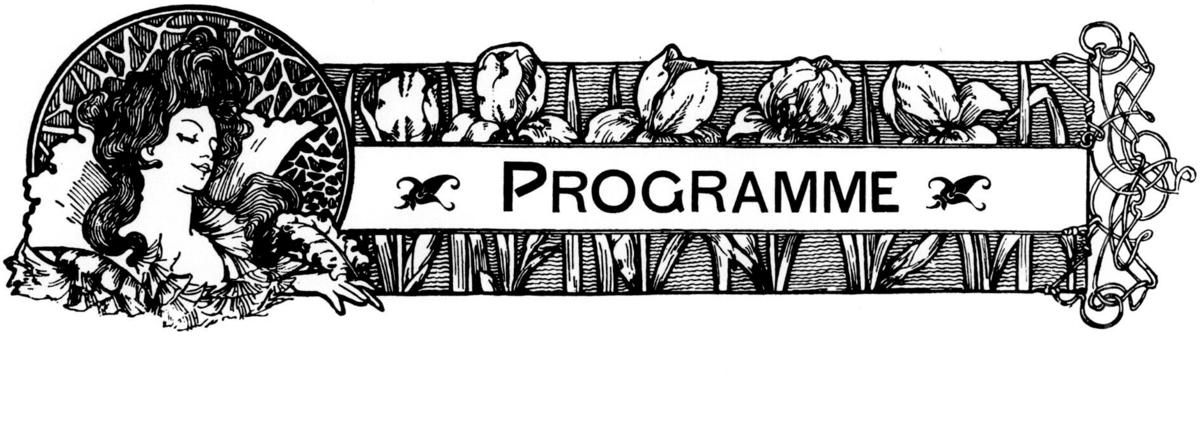
PROGRAMME

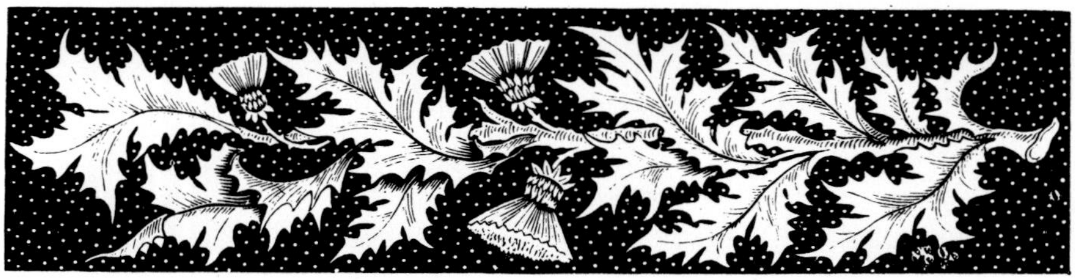

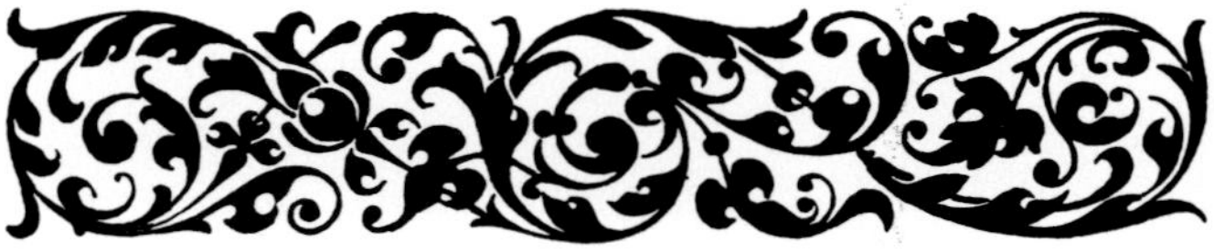

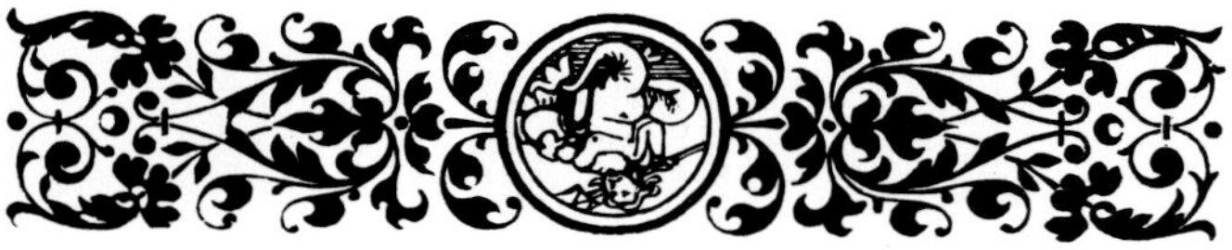

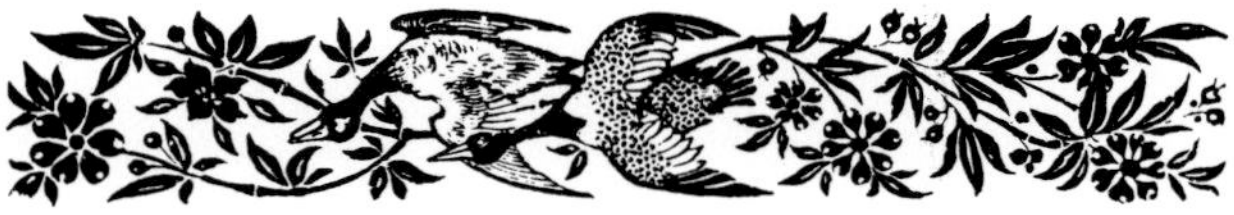

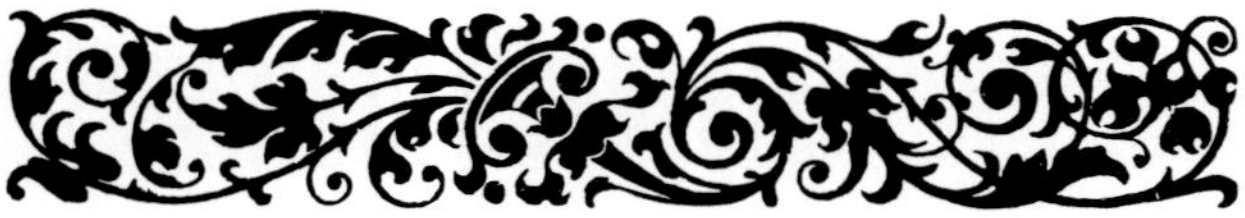

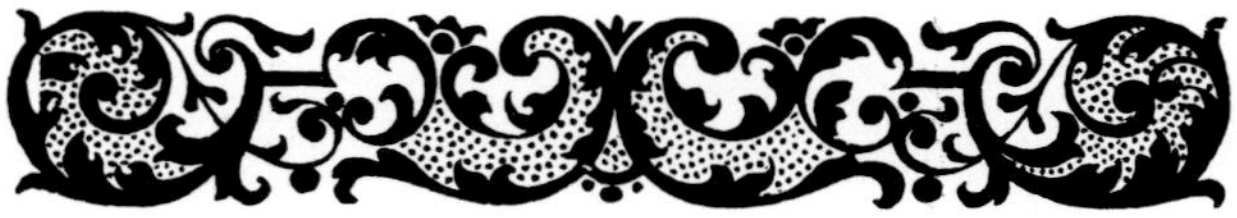

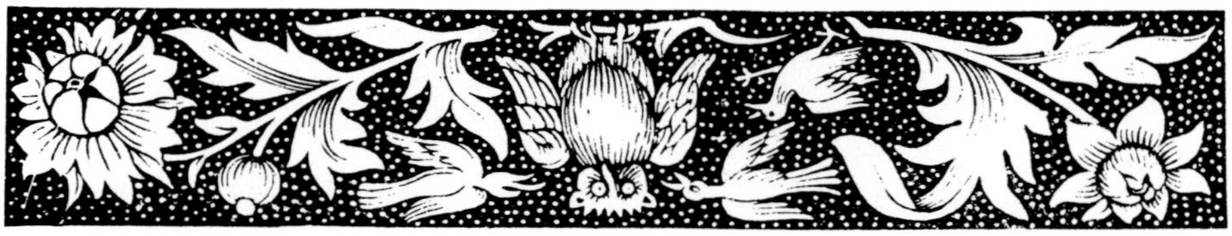

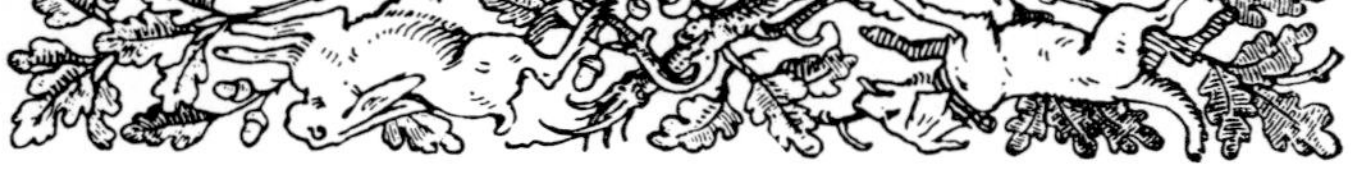

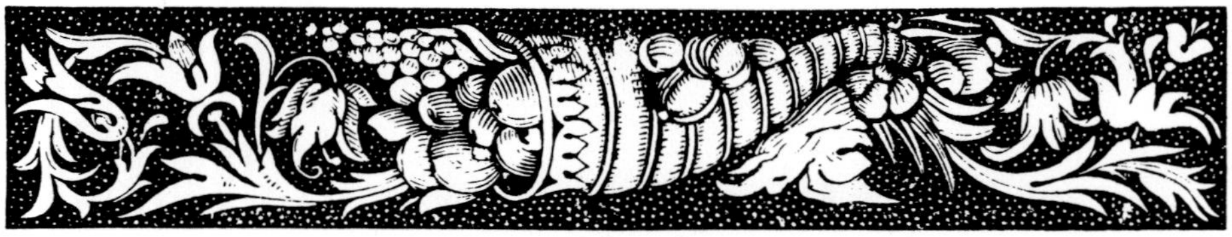

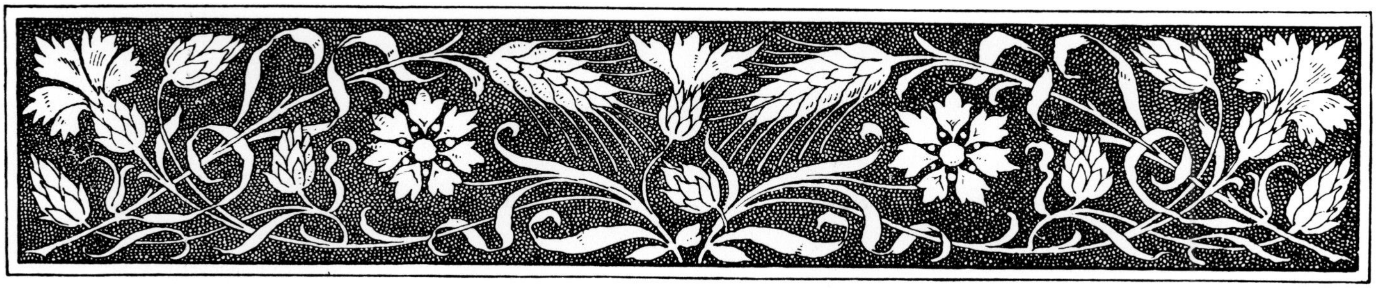

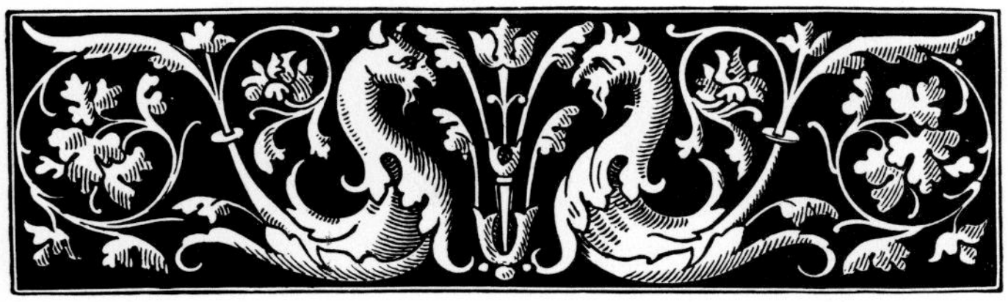

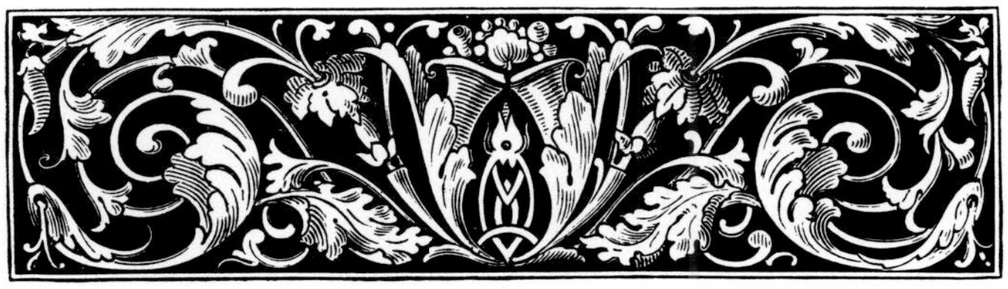

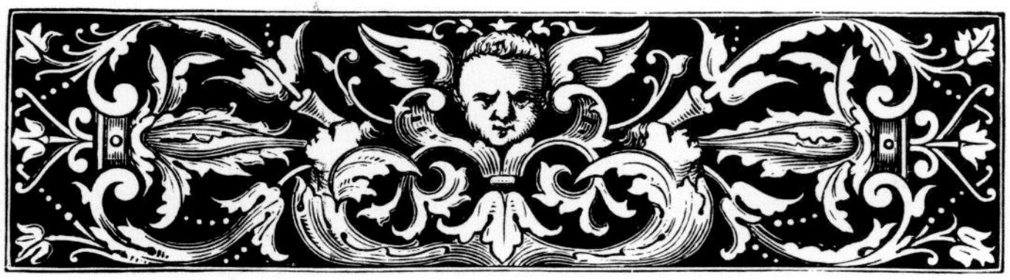

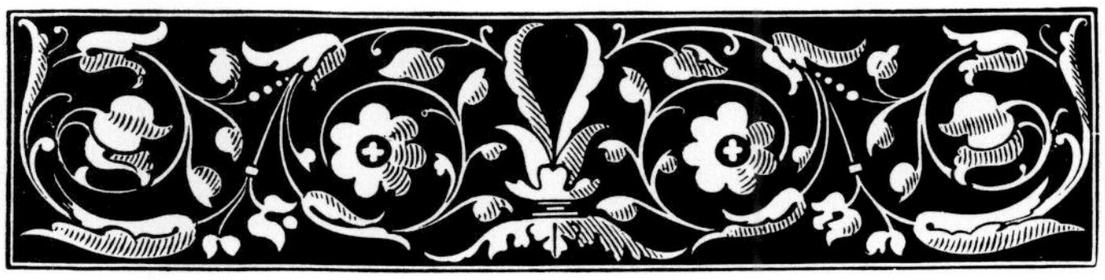

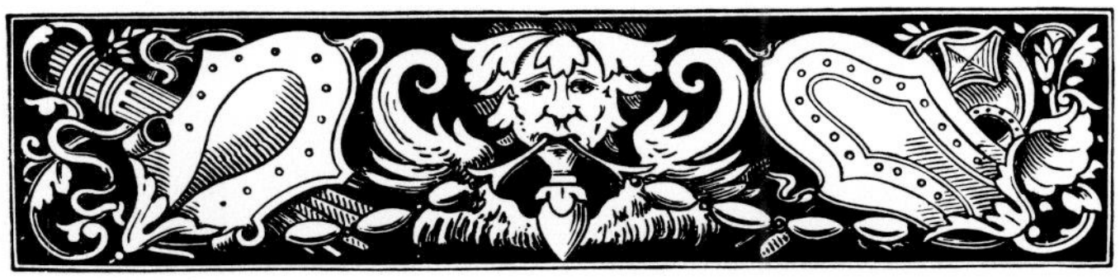

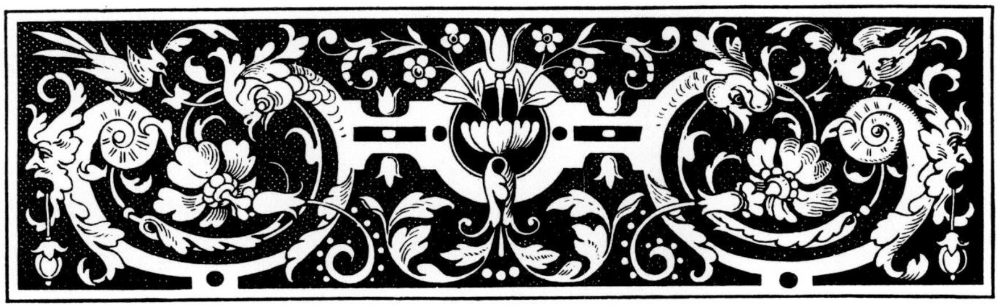

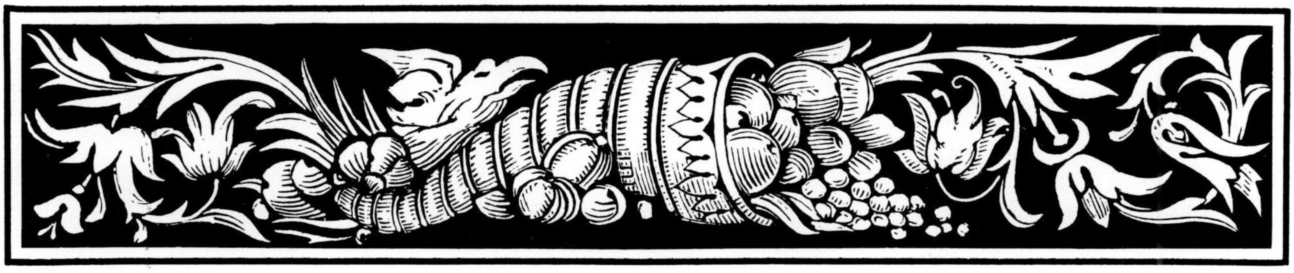

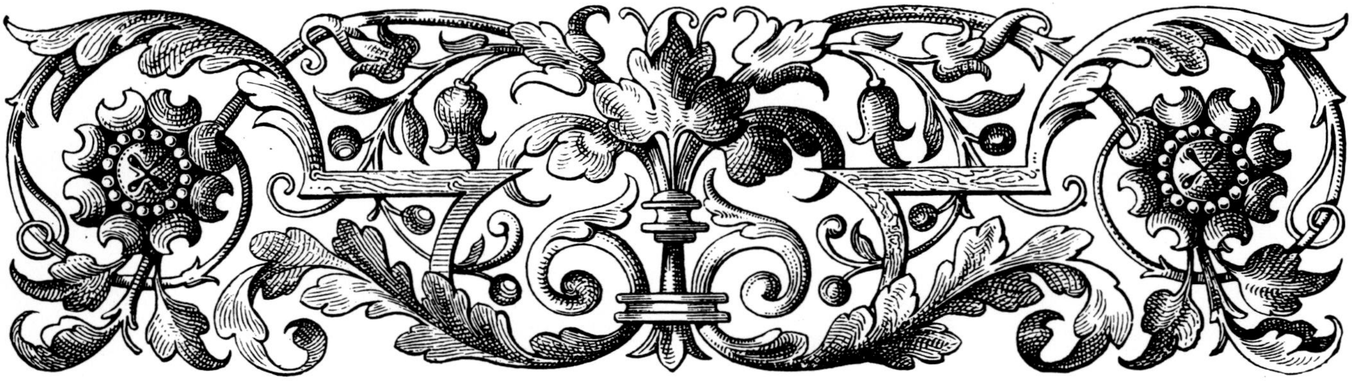

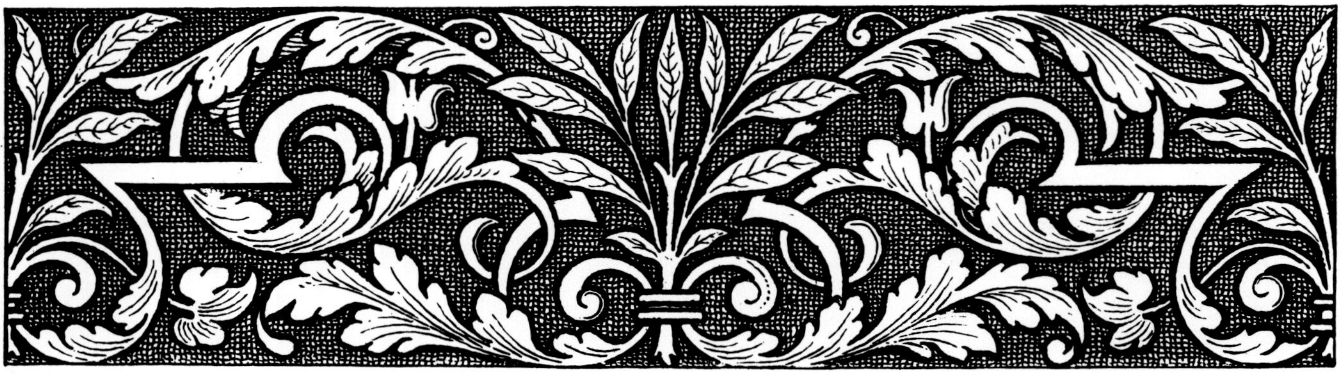

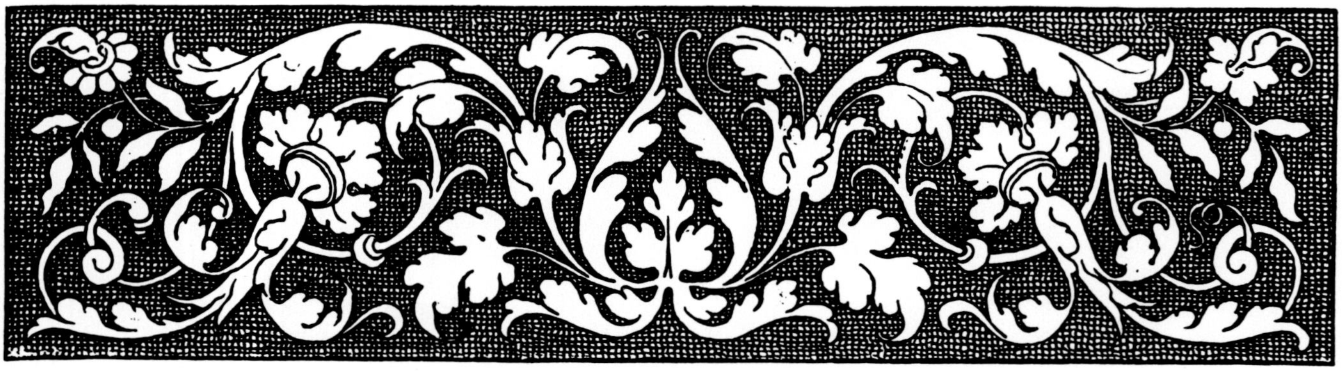